# Vintage Homes



## *COLORING BOOK FOR ADULTS AND KIDS*

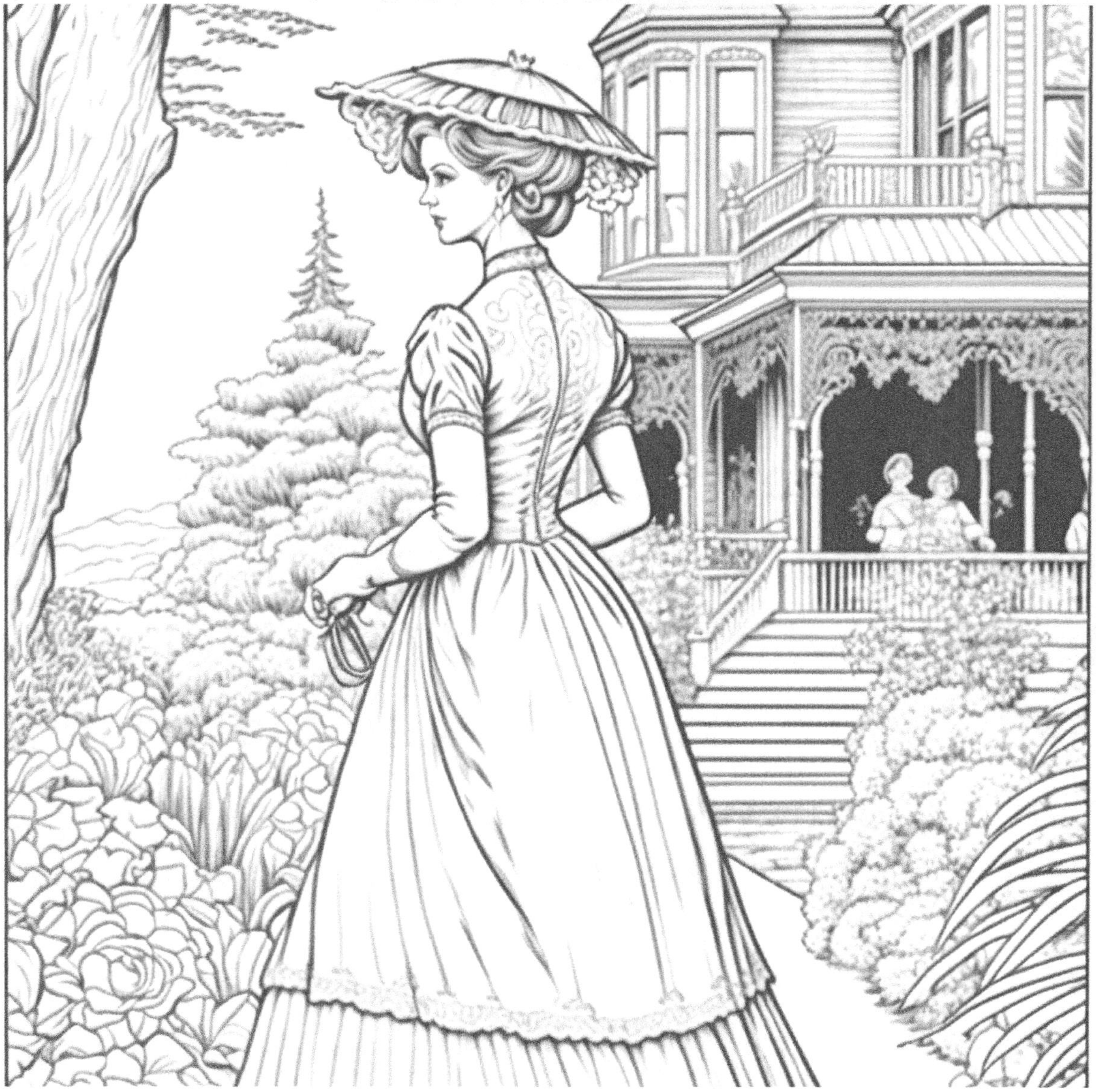

The Sunset

NOTEBOOKS AND BOOKS DESIGNING

# COLOR TEST PAGE

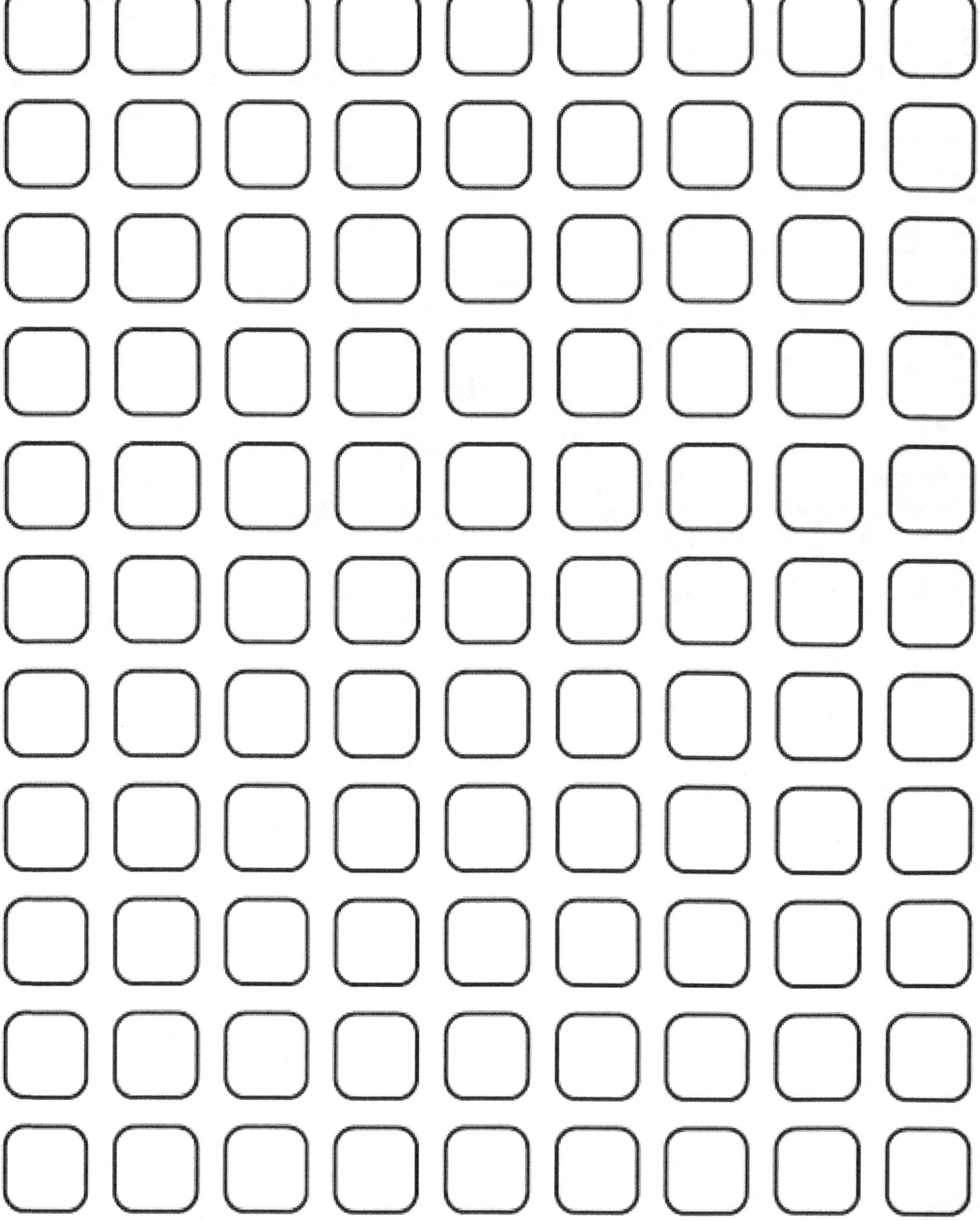

*This Book belongs to:*

..........................................

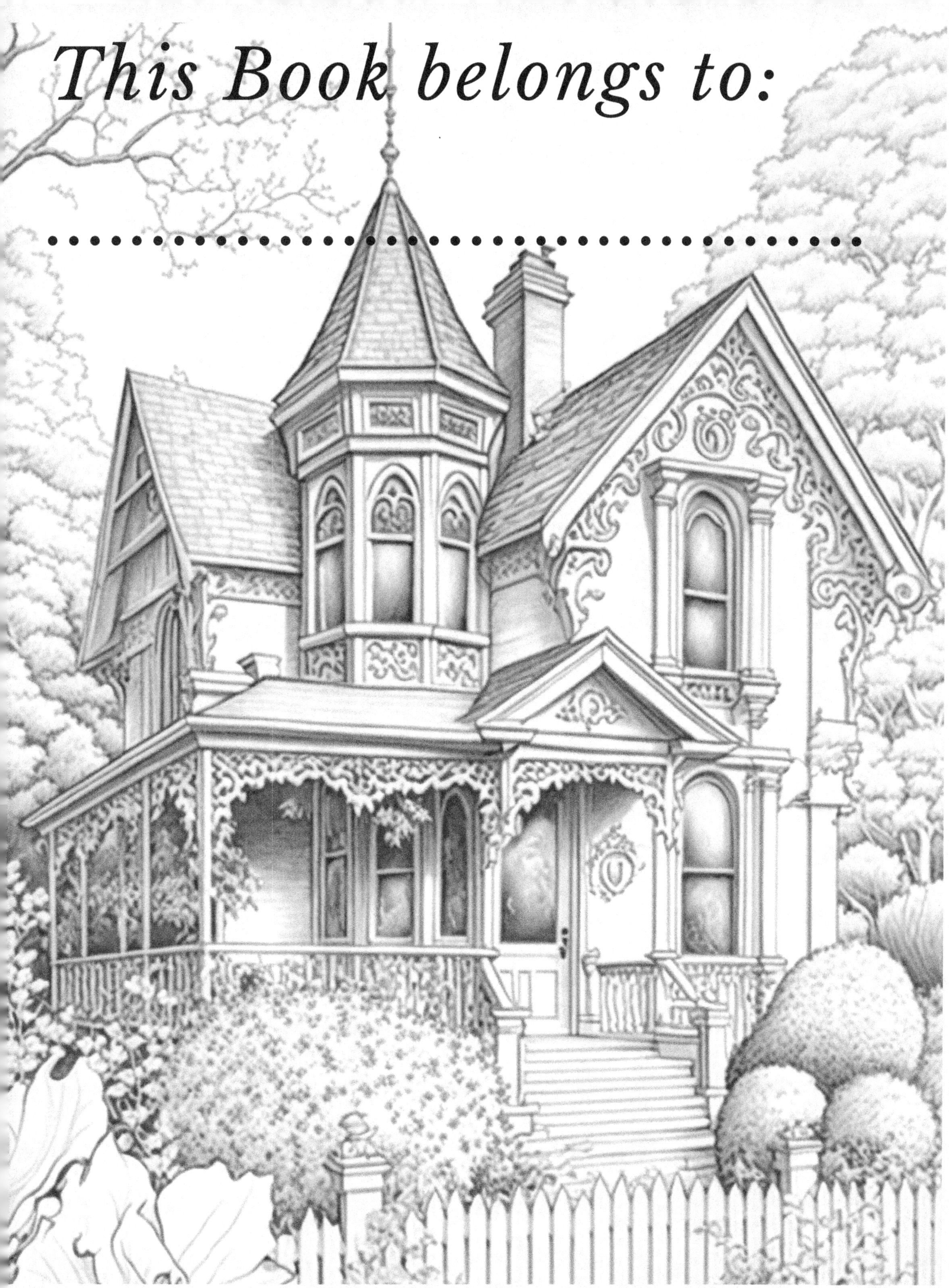

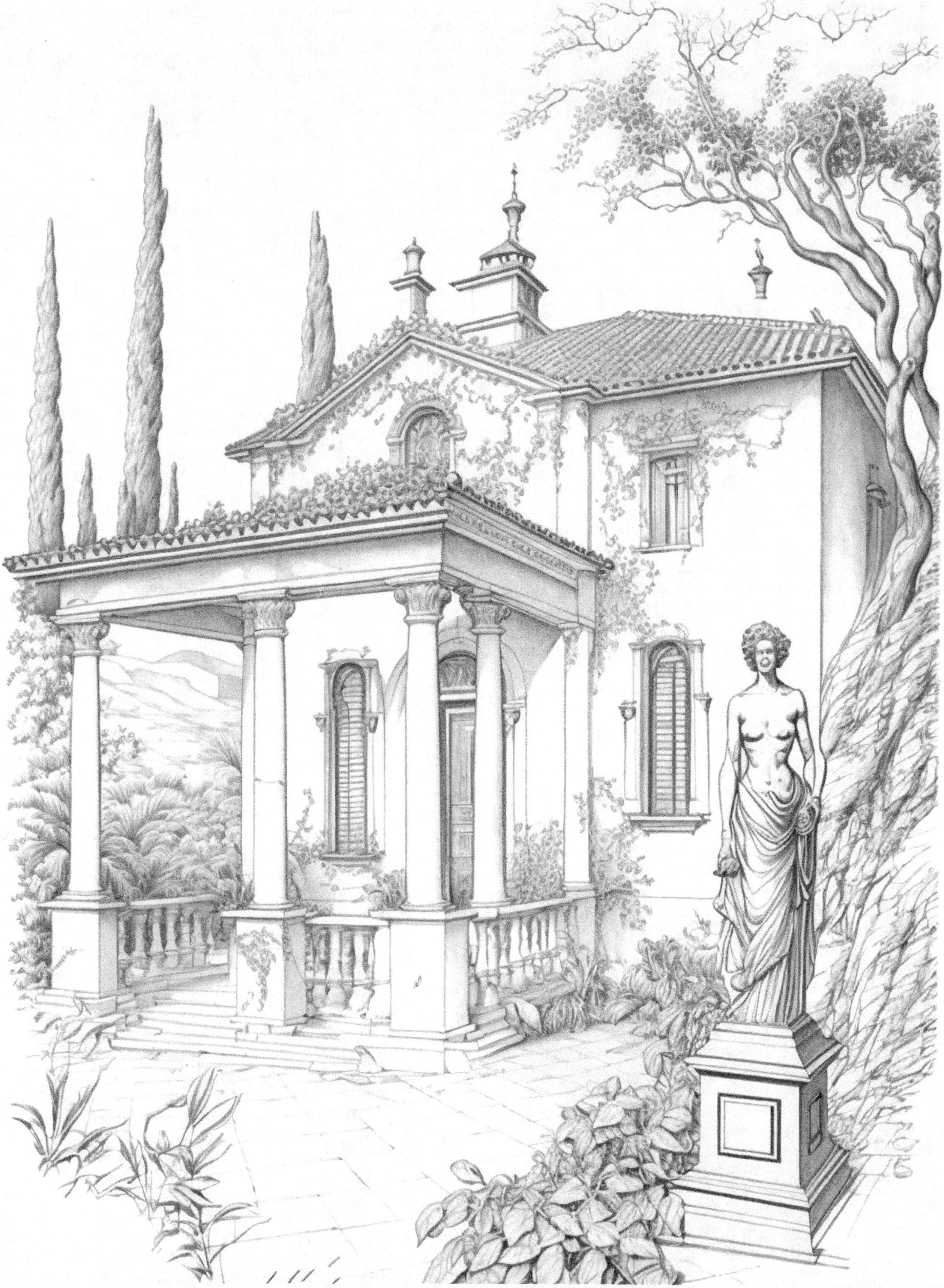

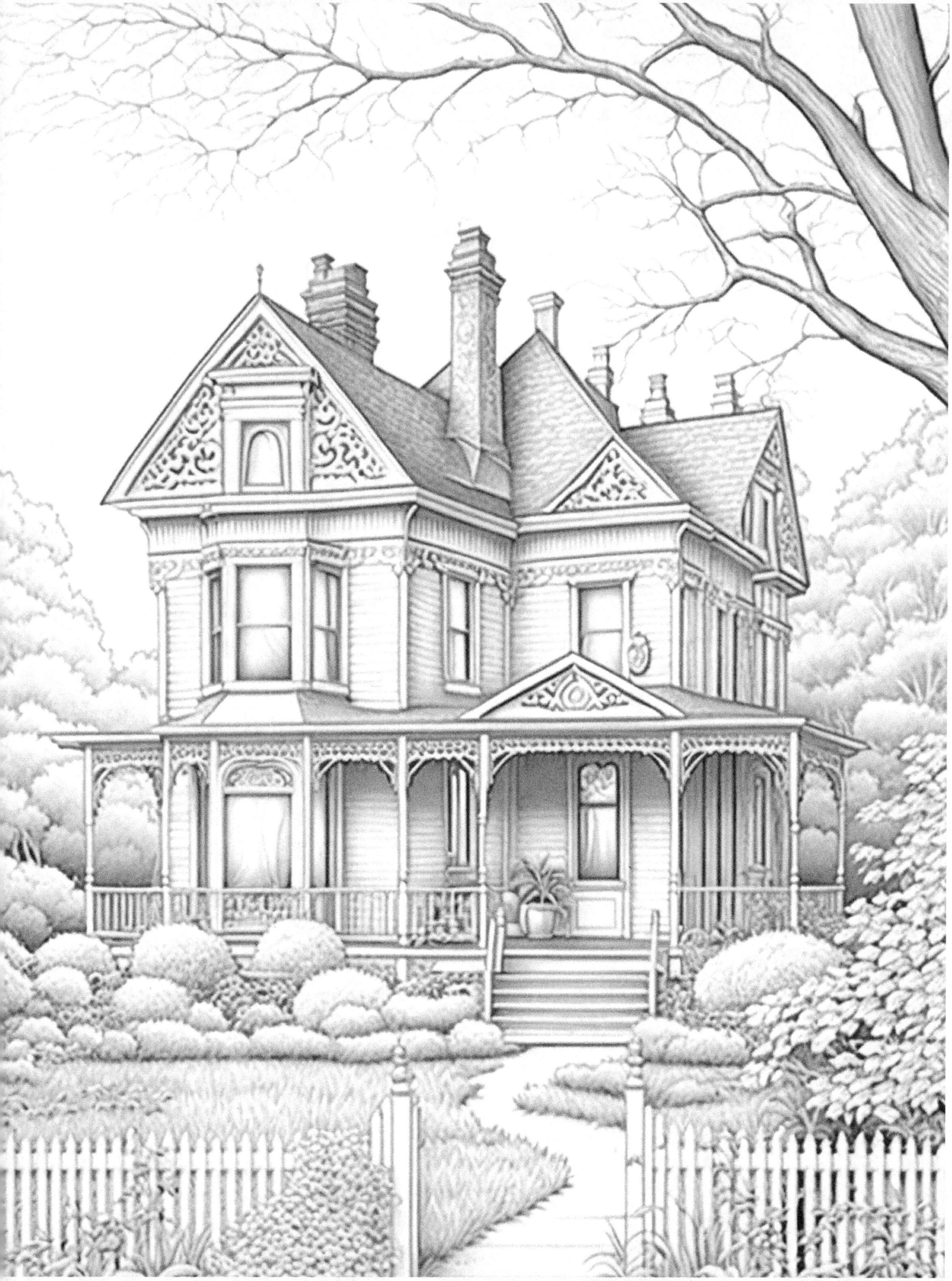

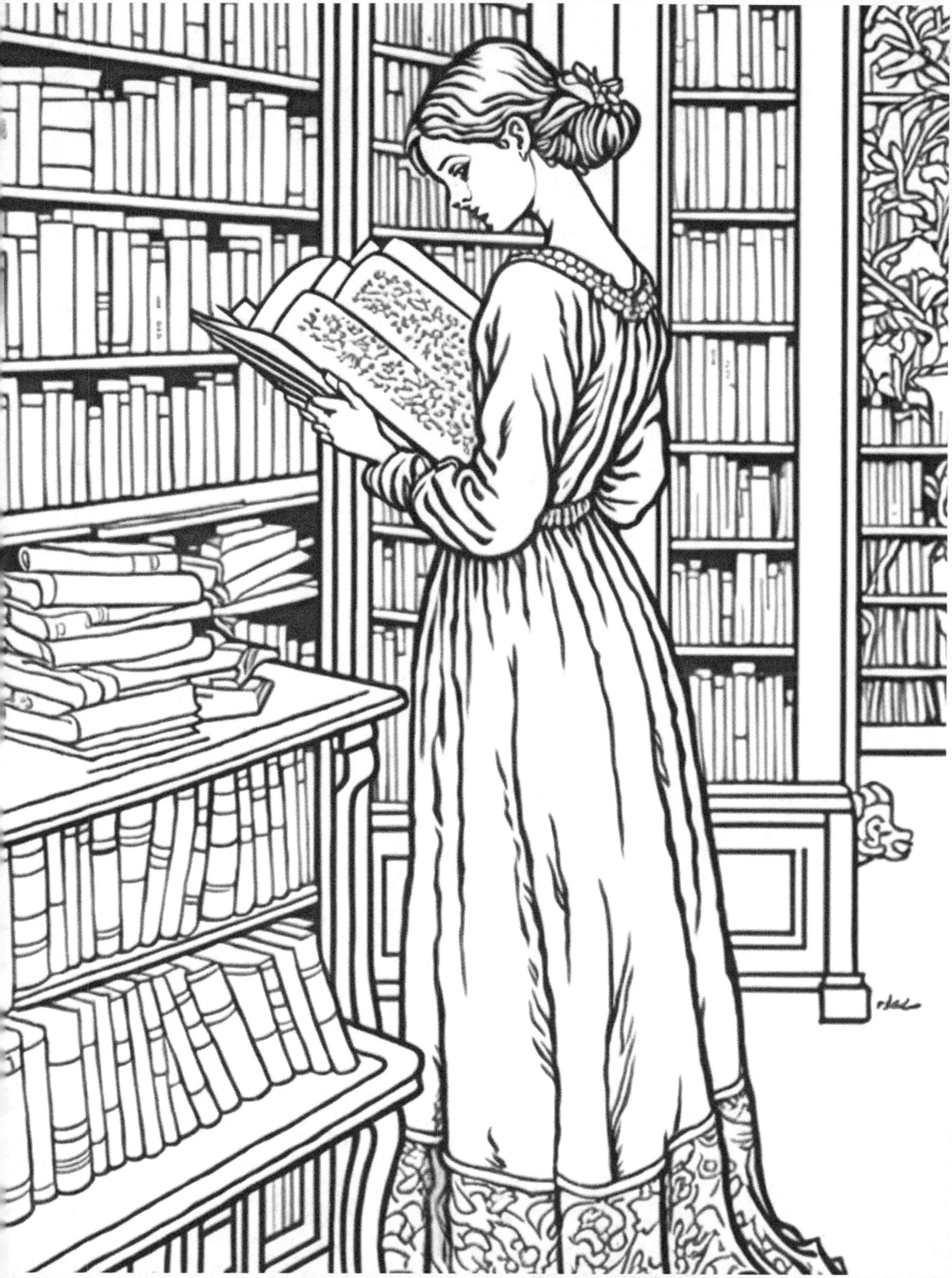

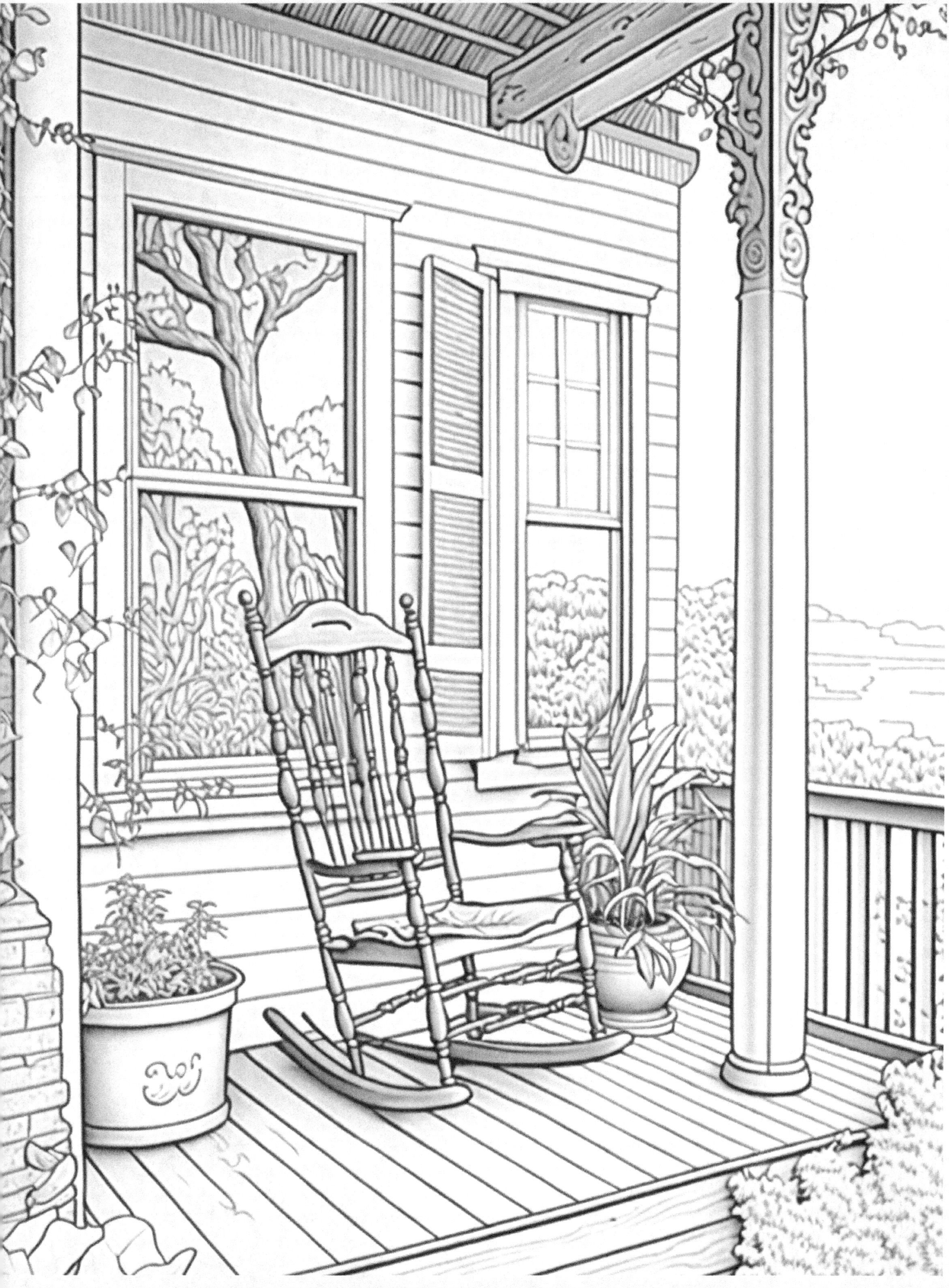

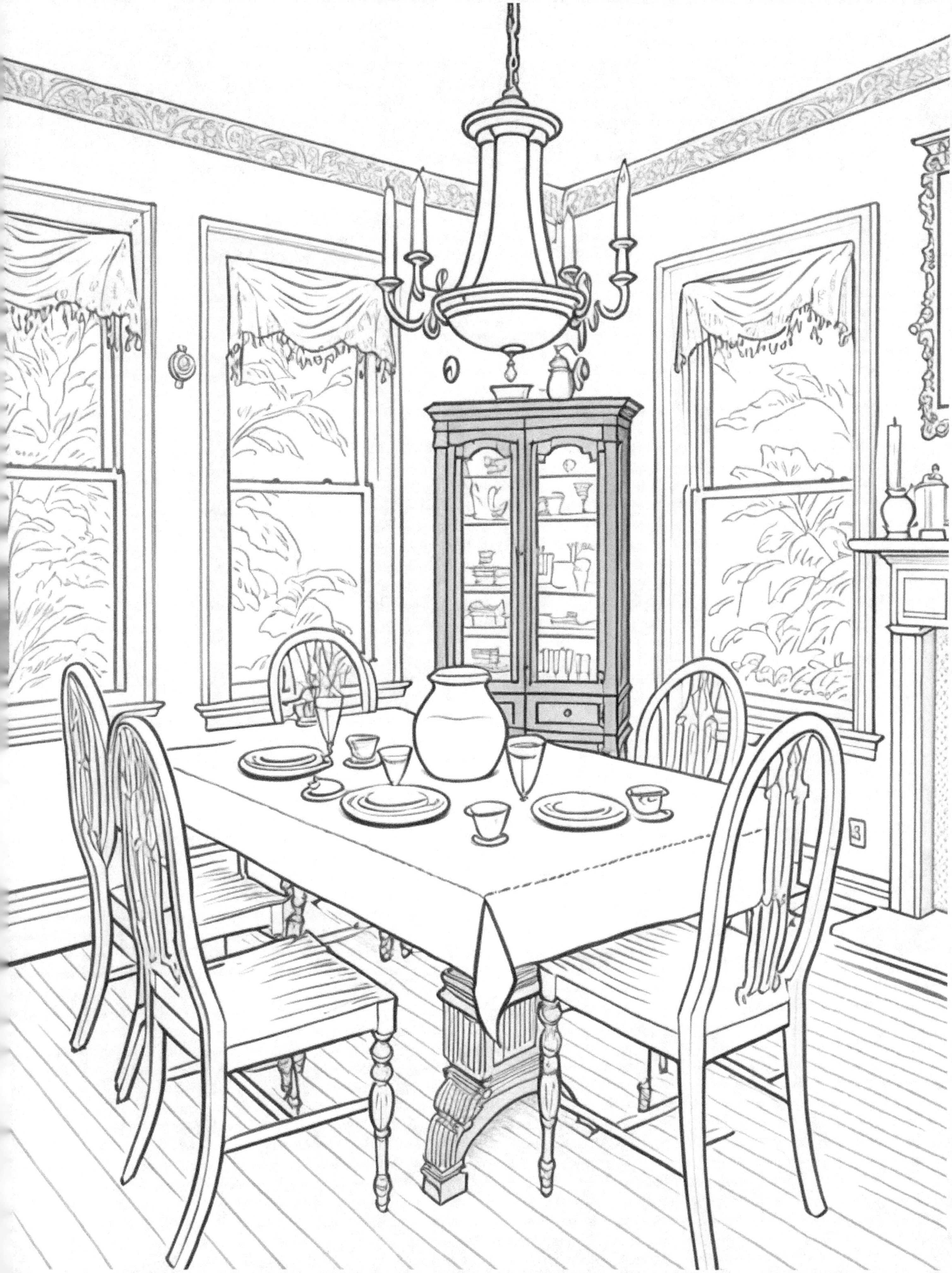

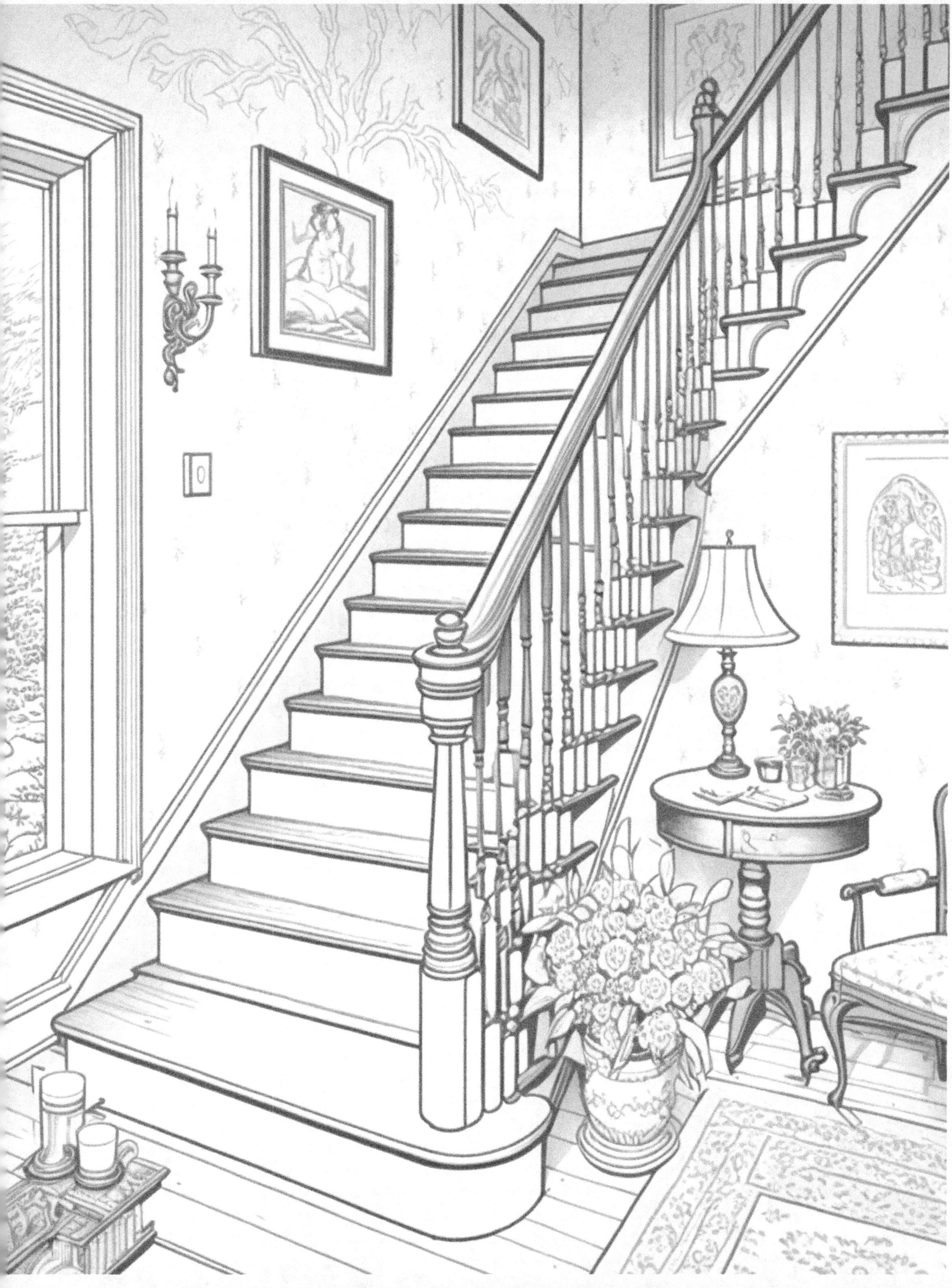

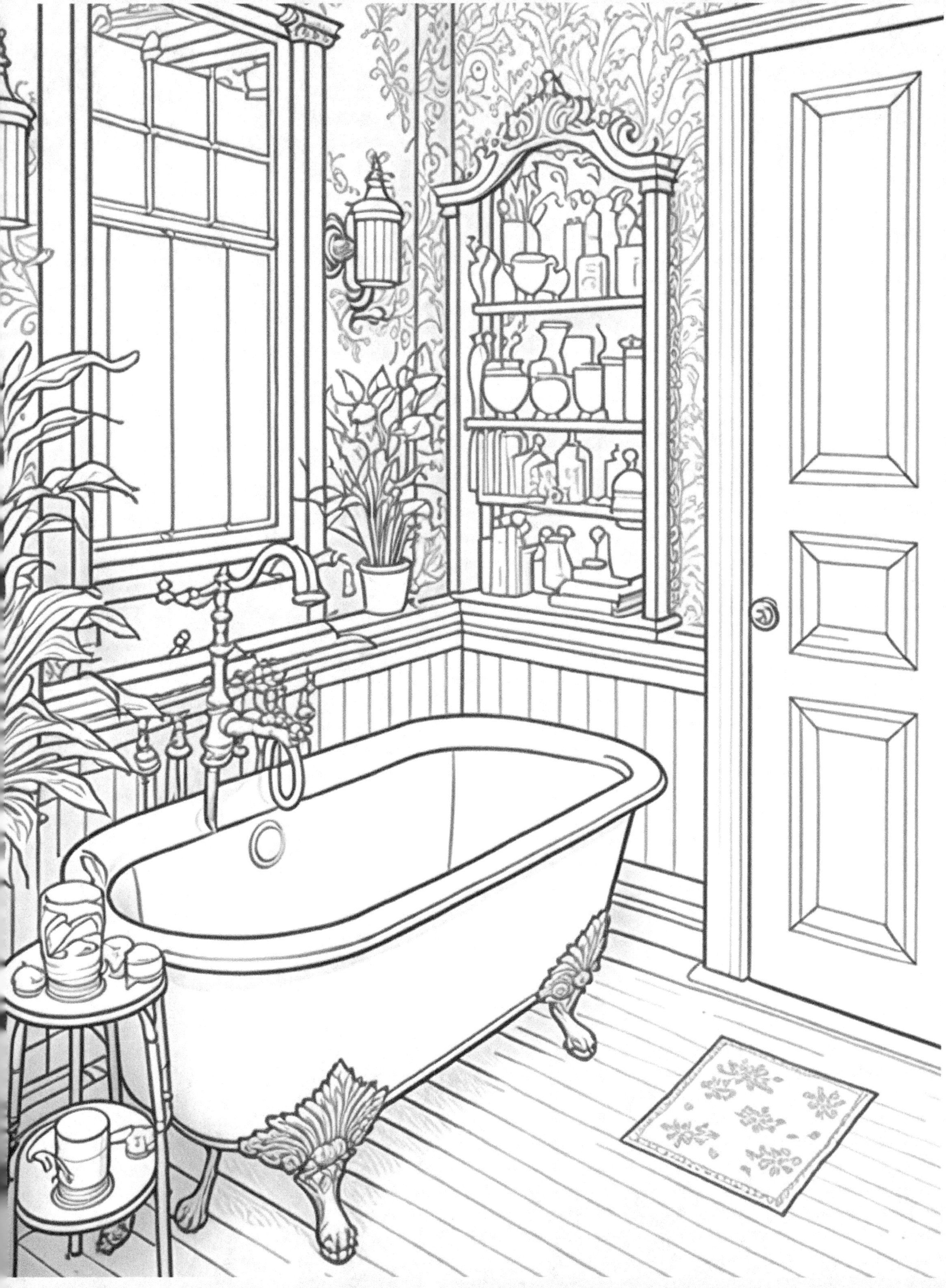

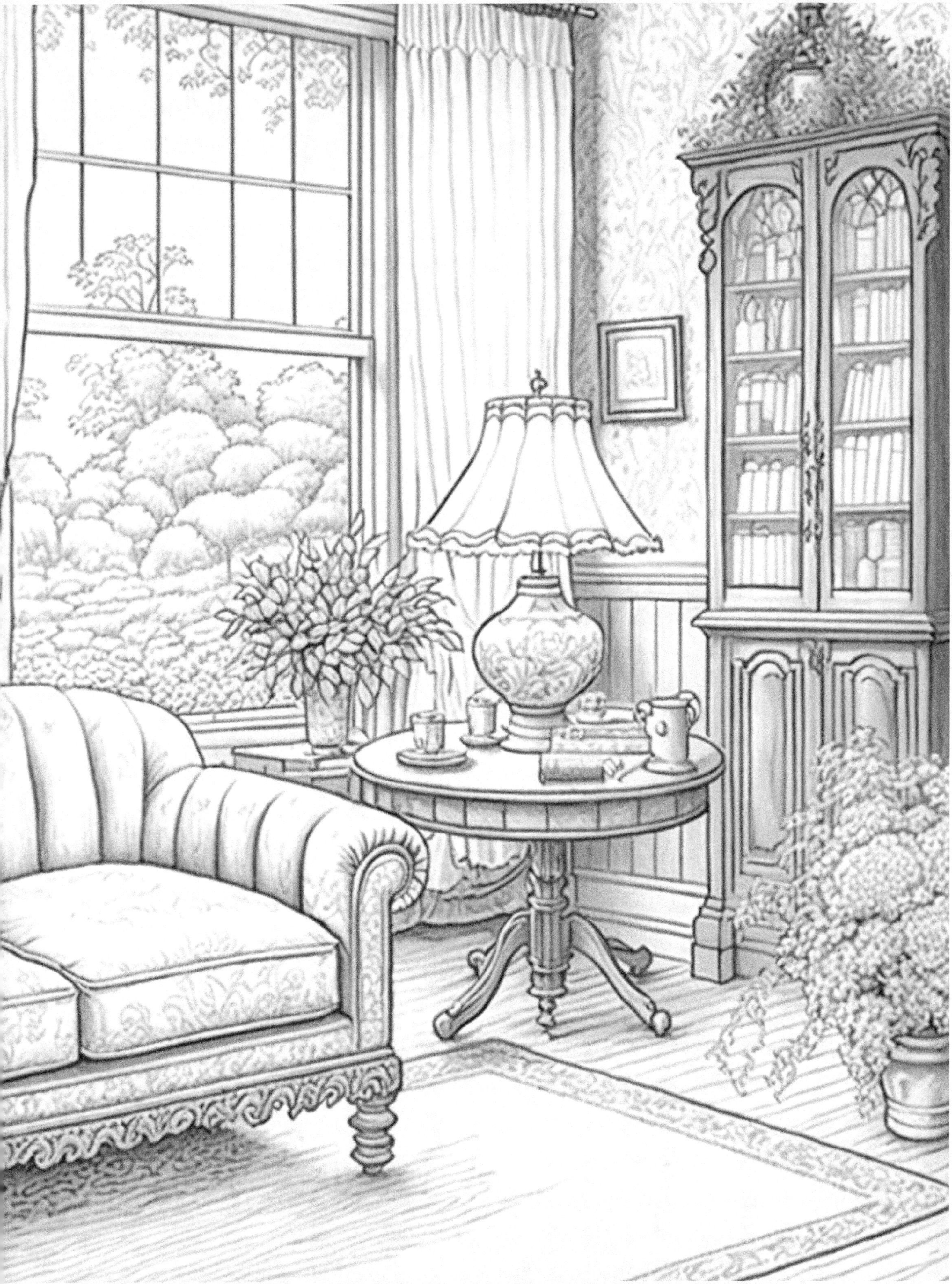

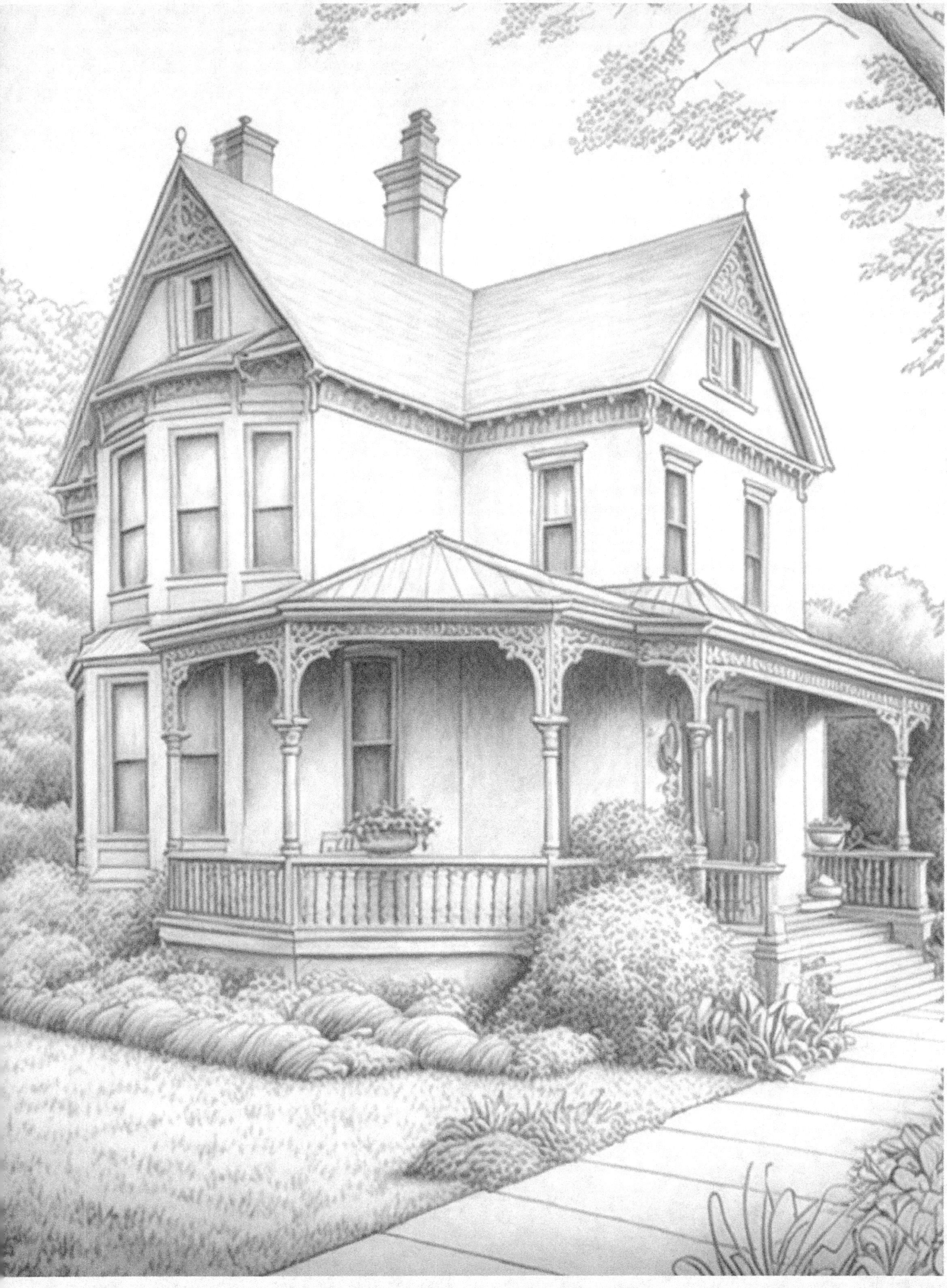

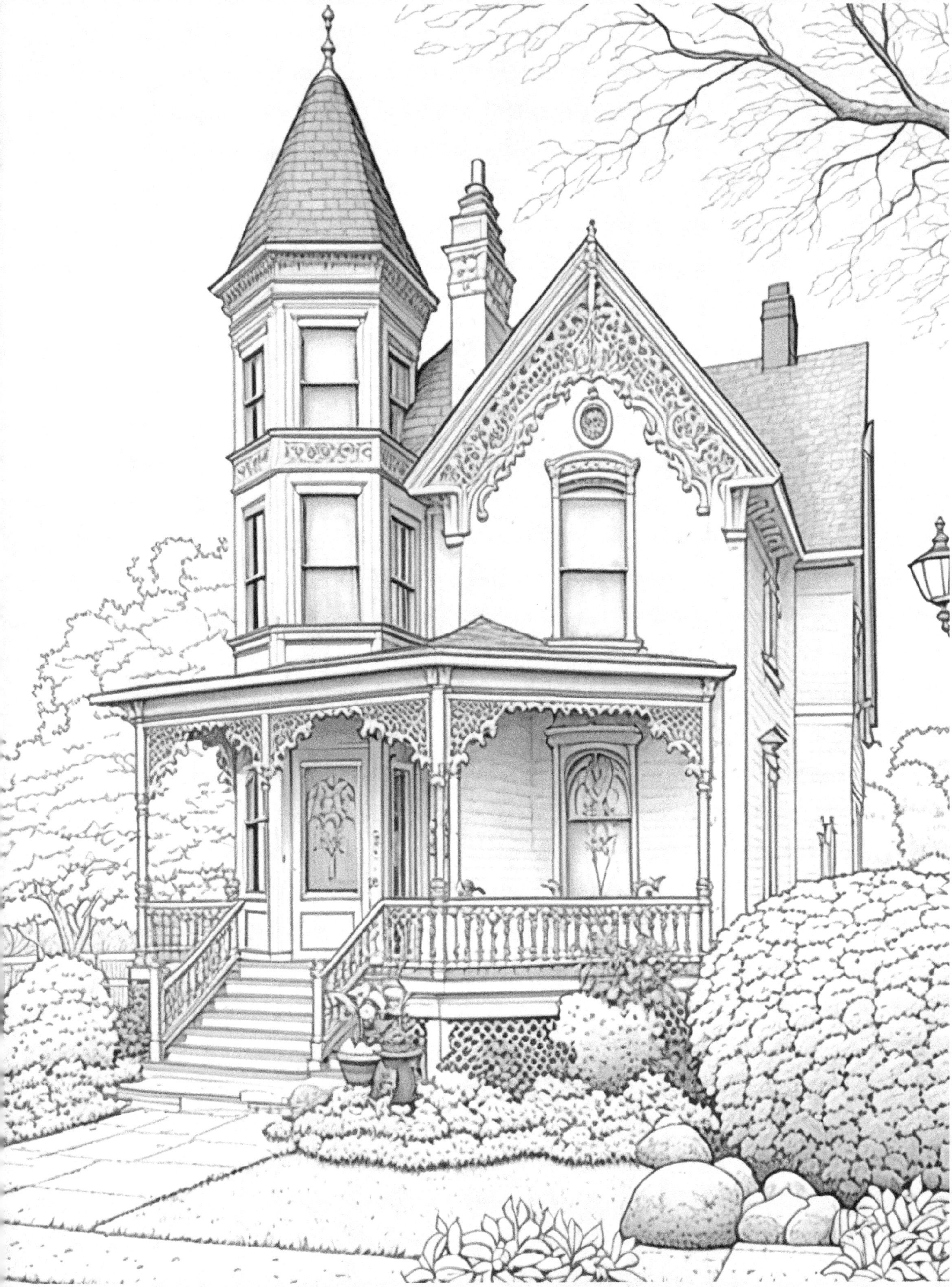

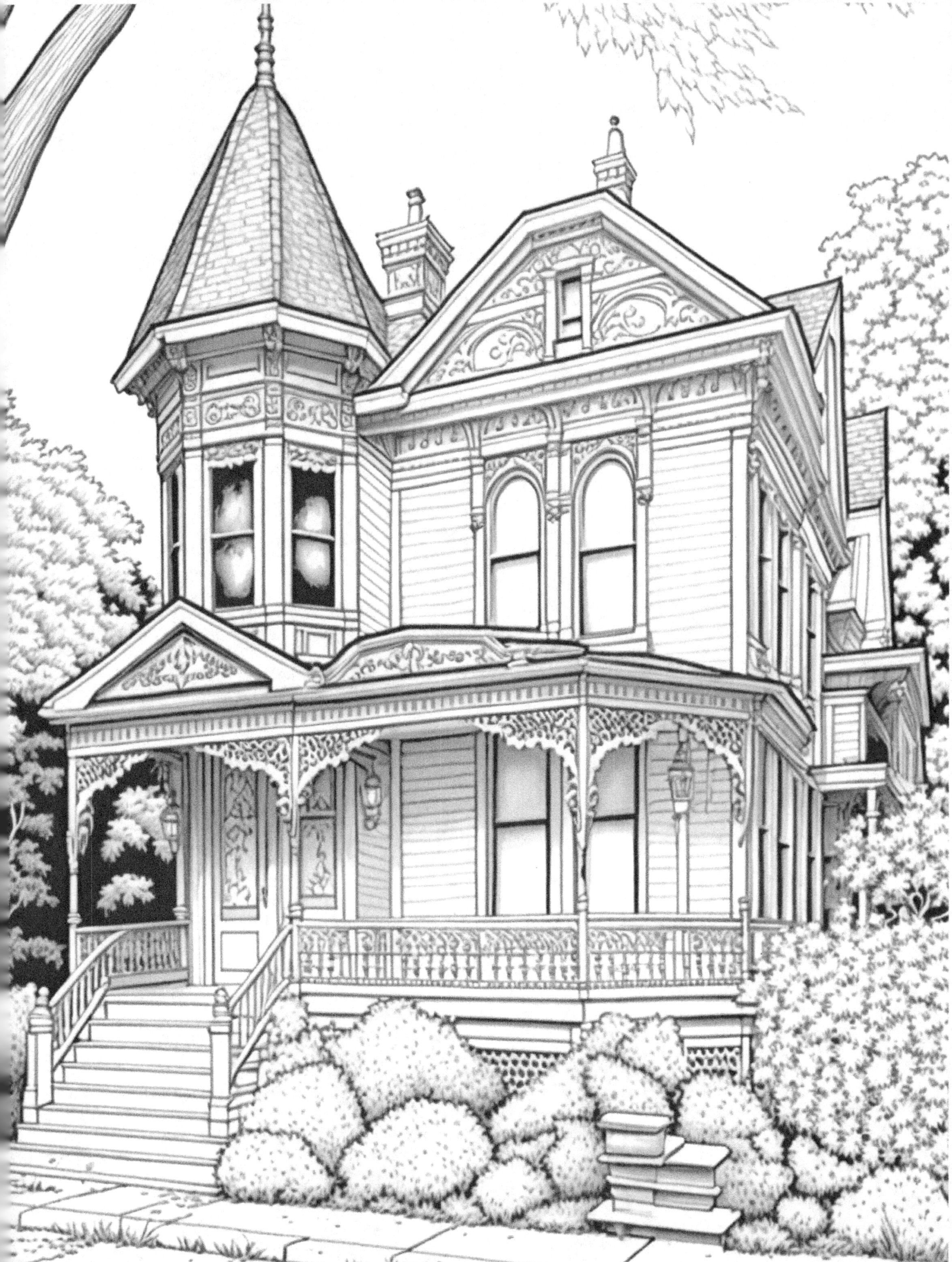

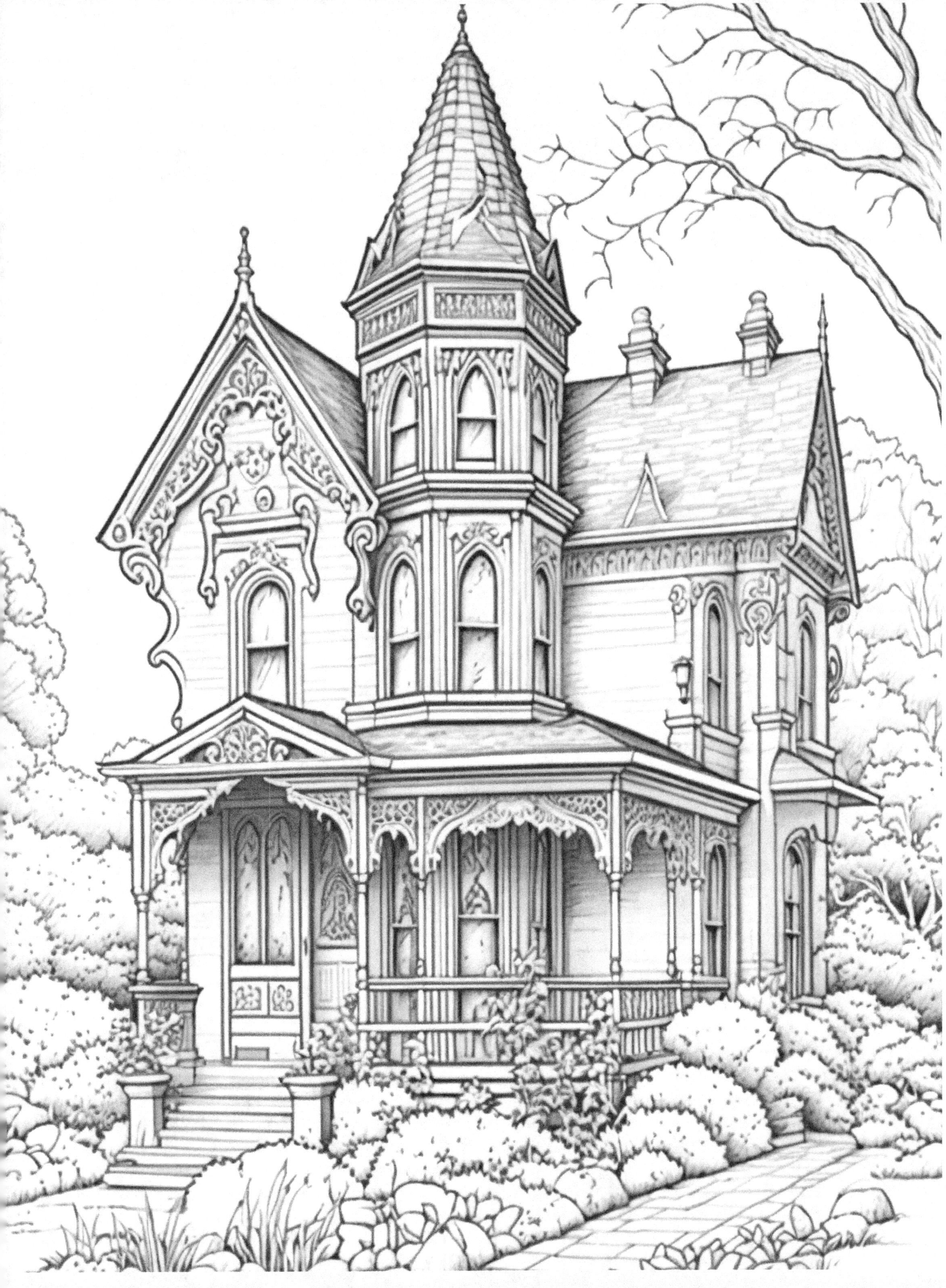

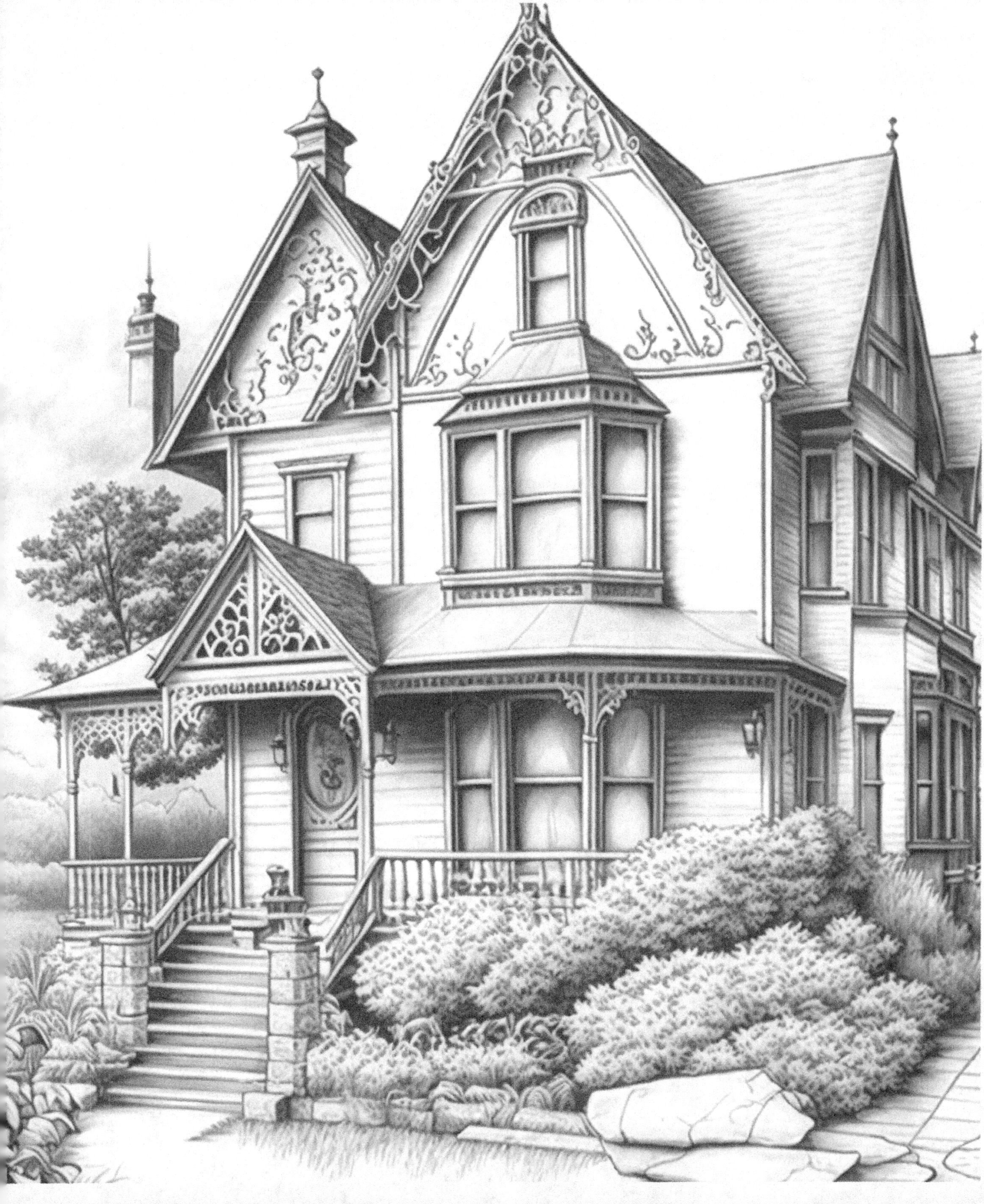

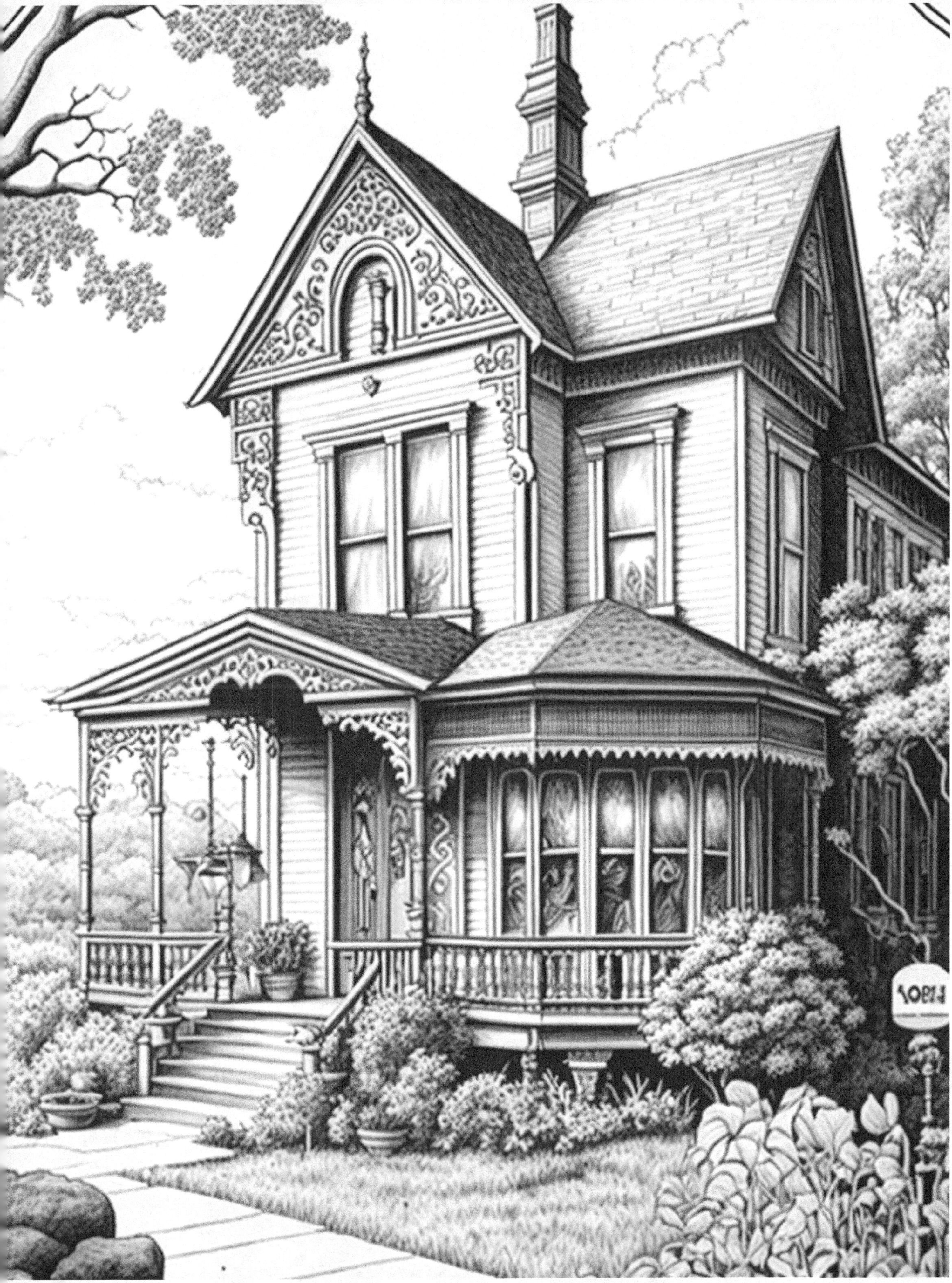

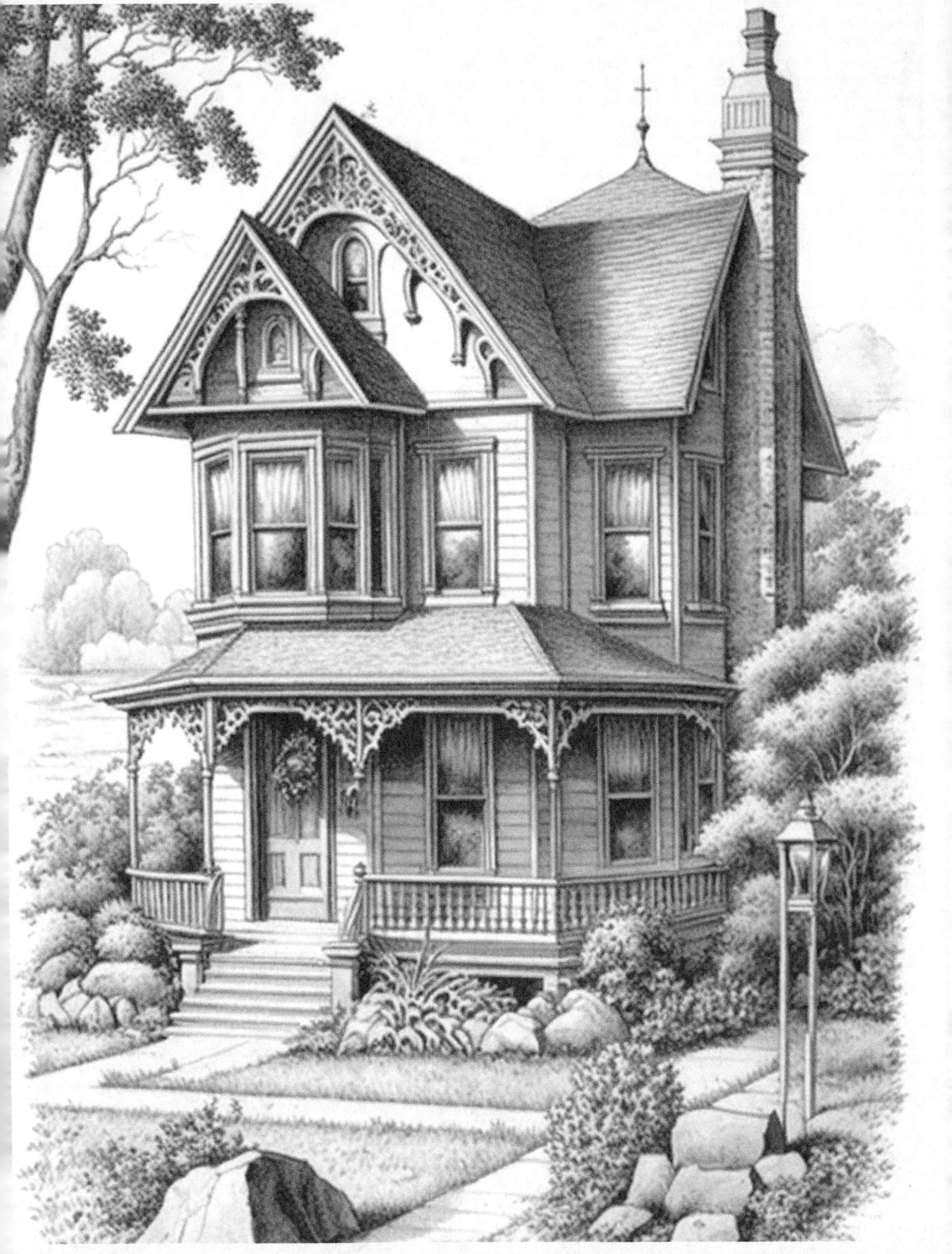

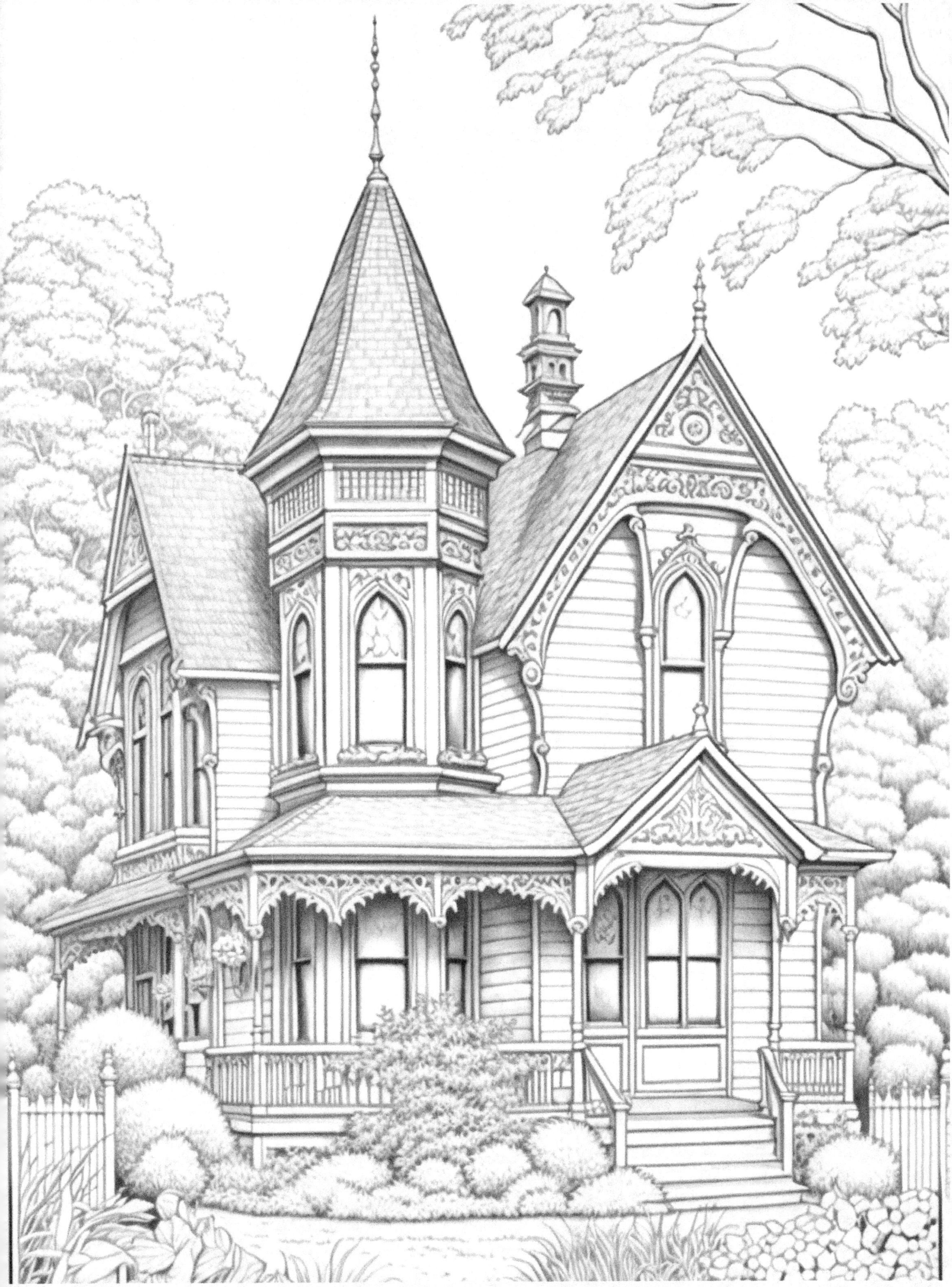

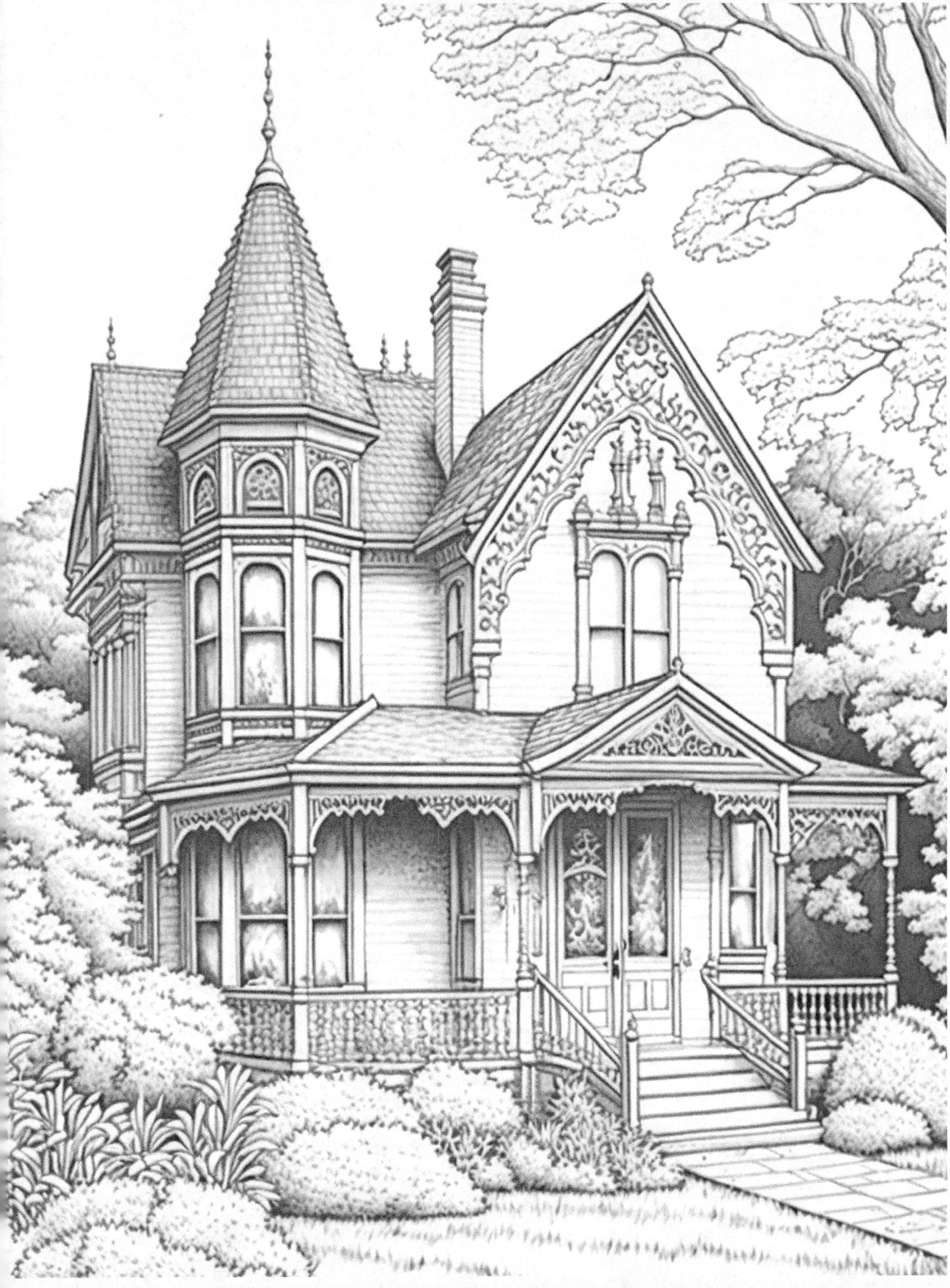

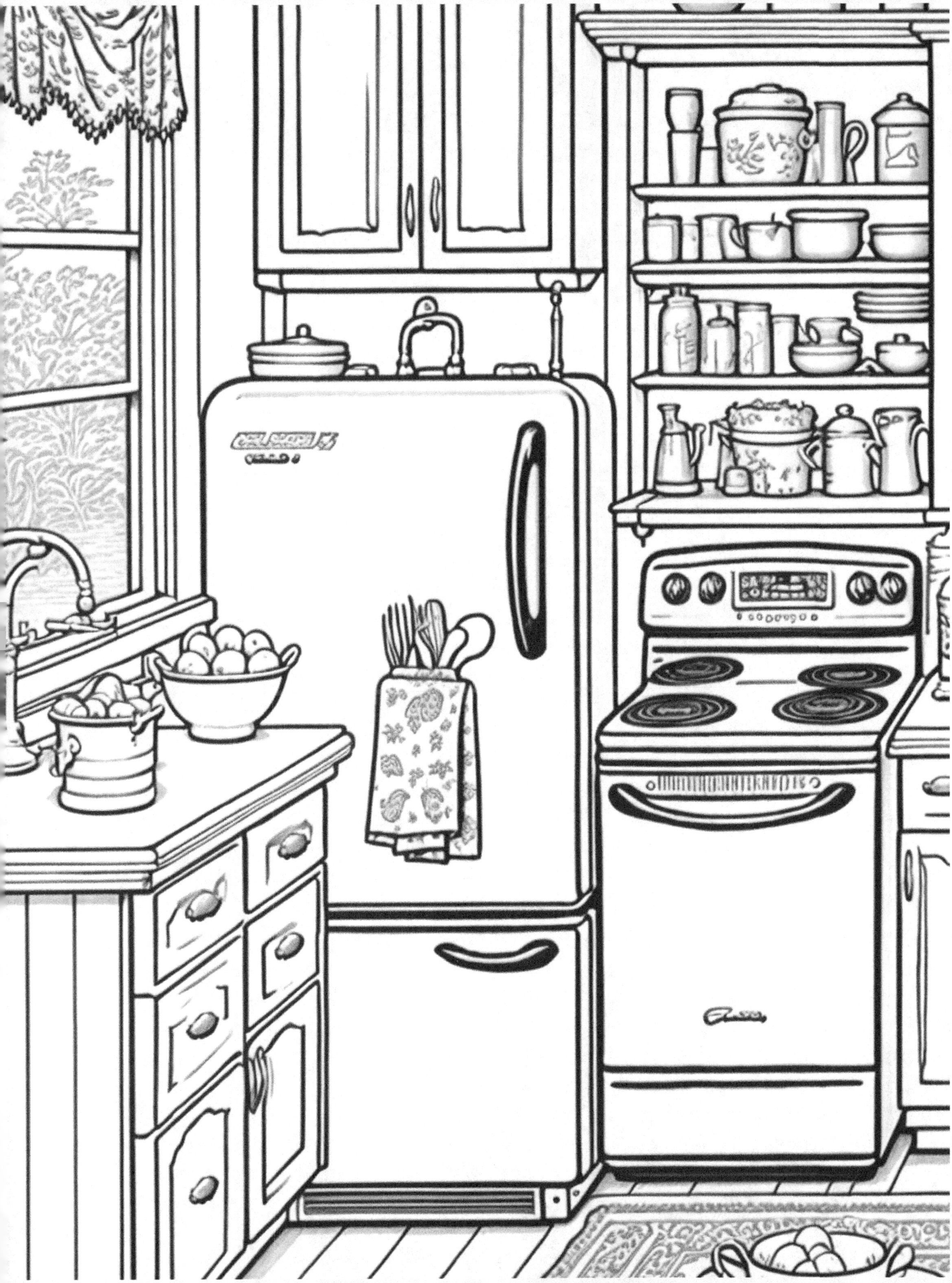

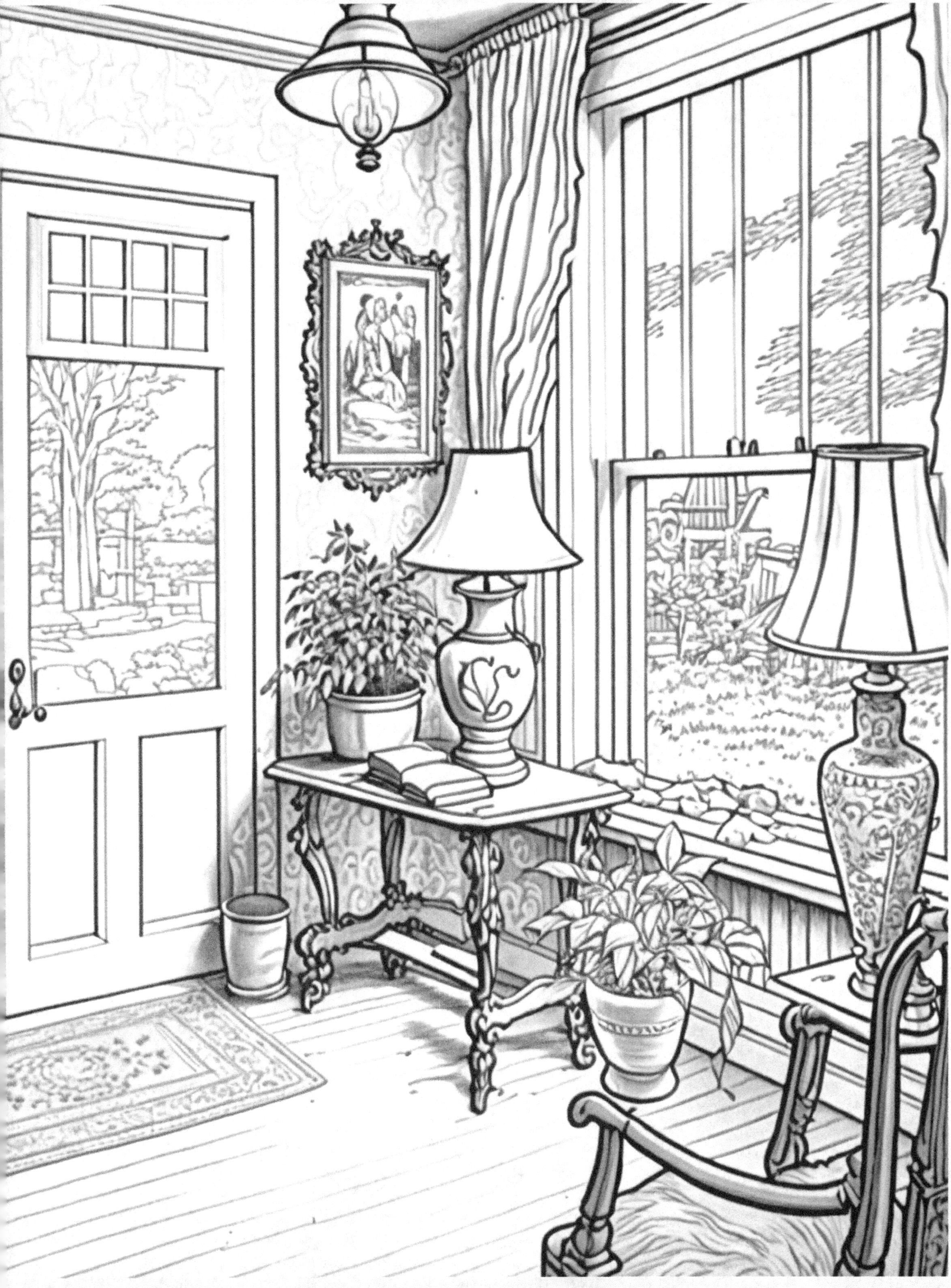

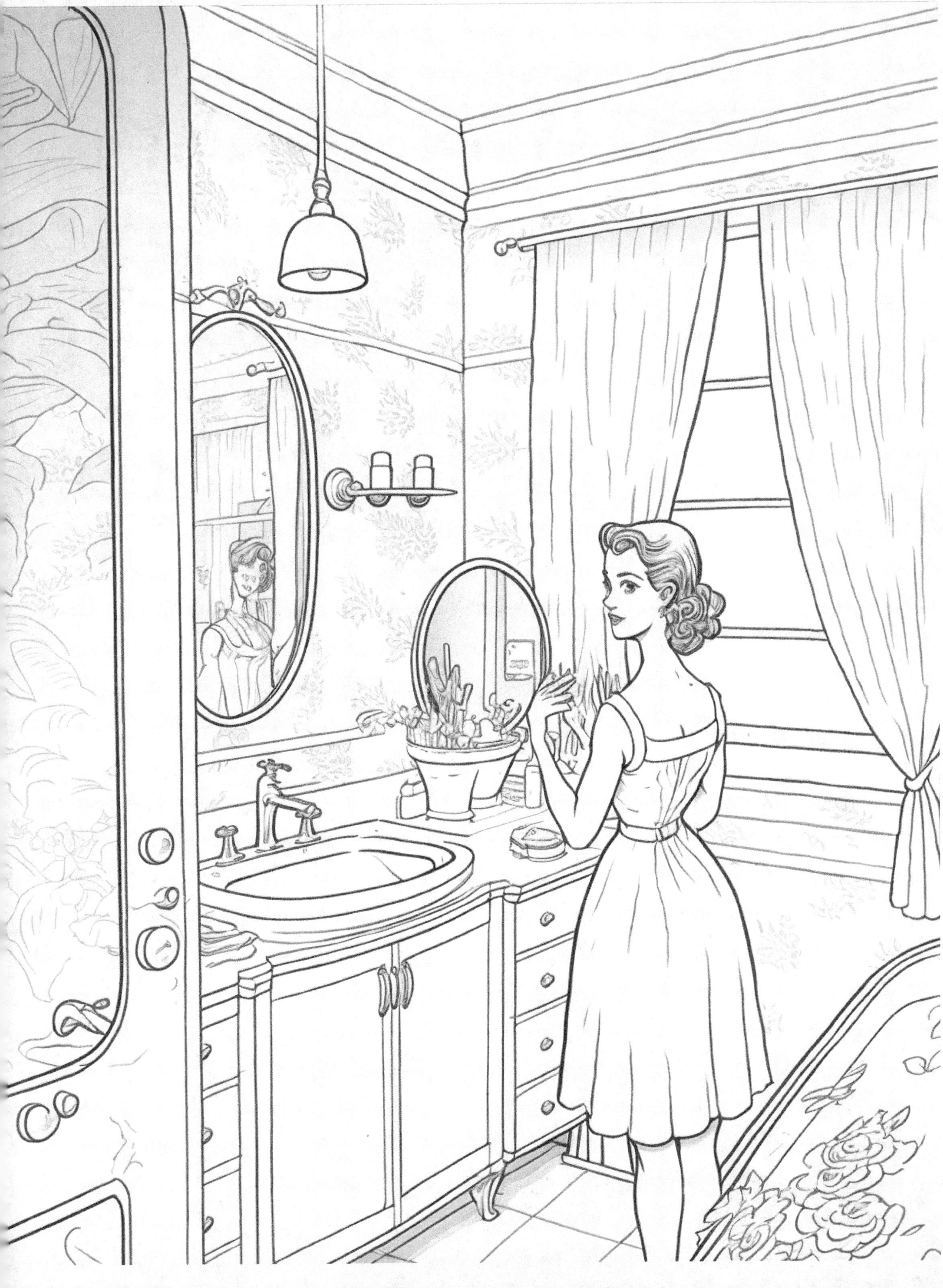

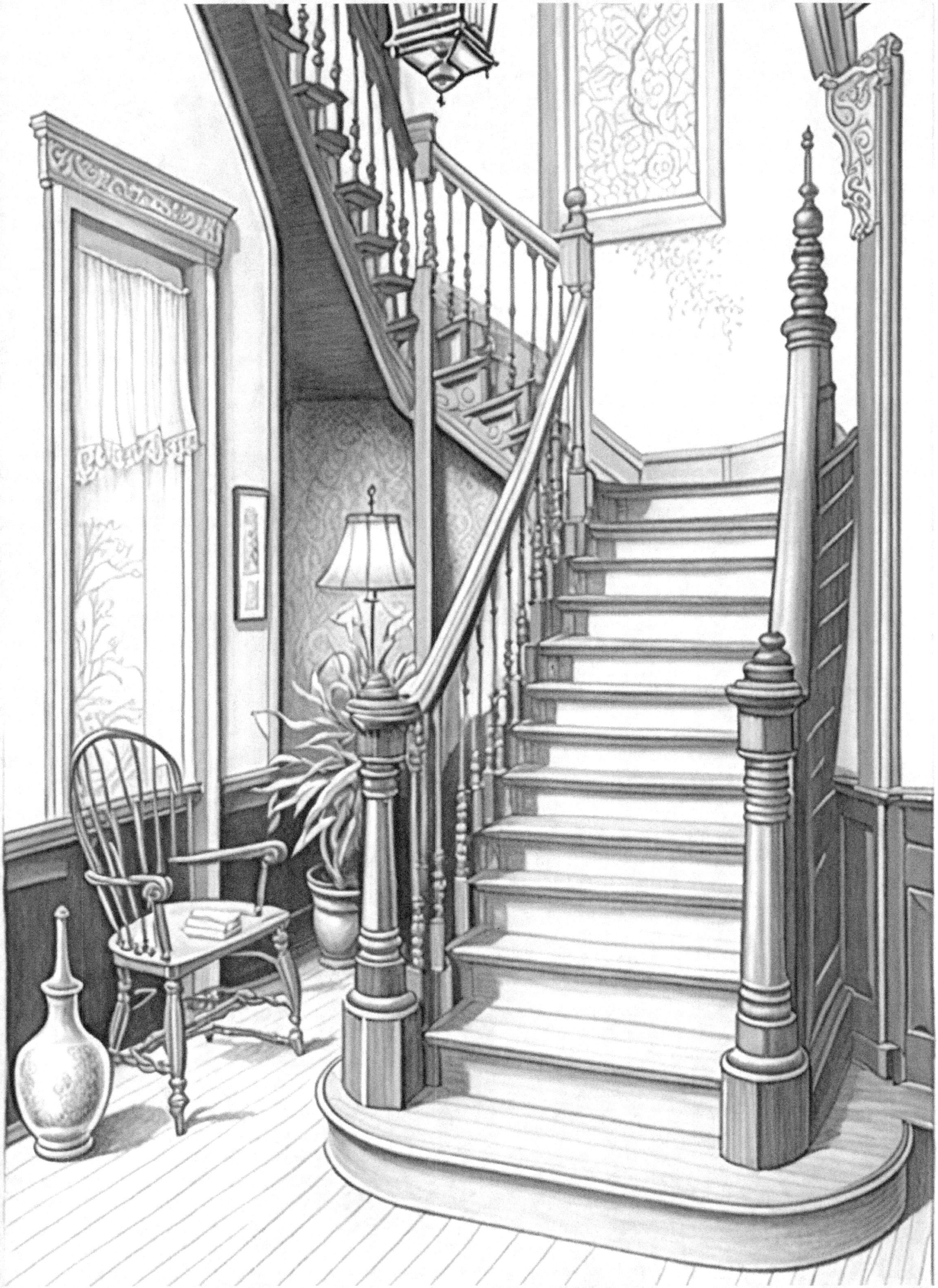

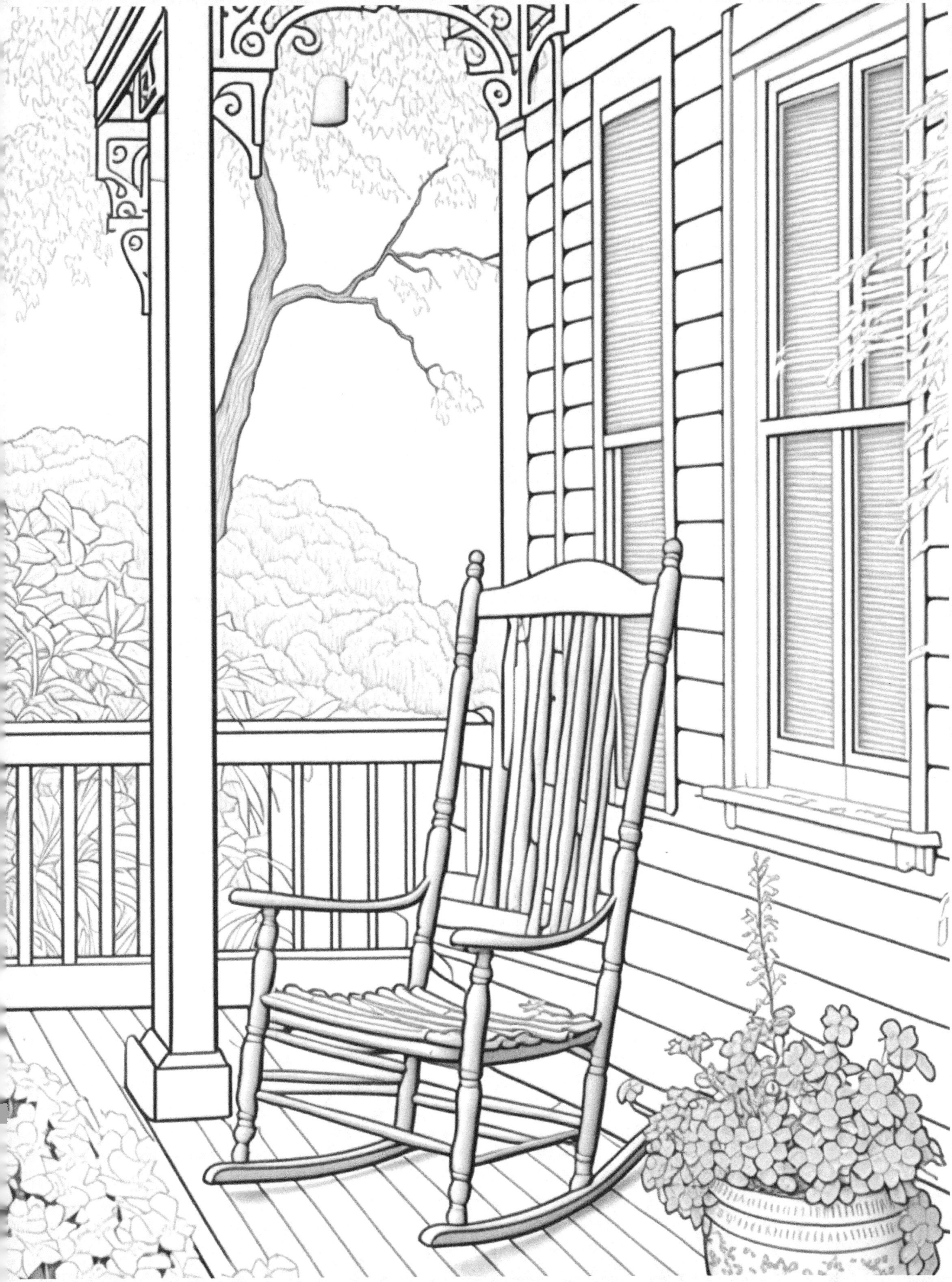

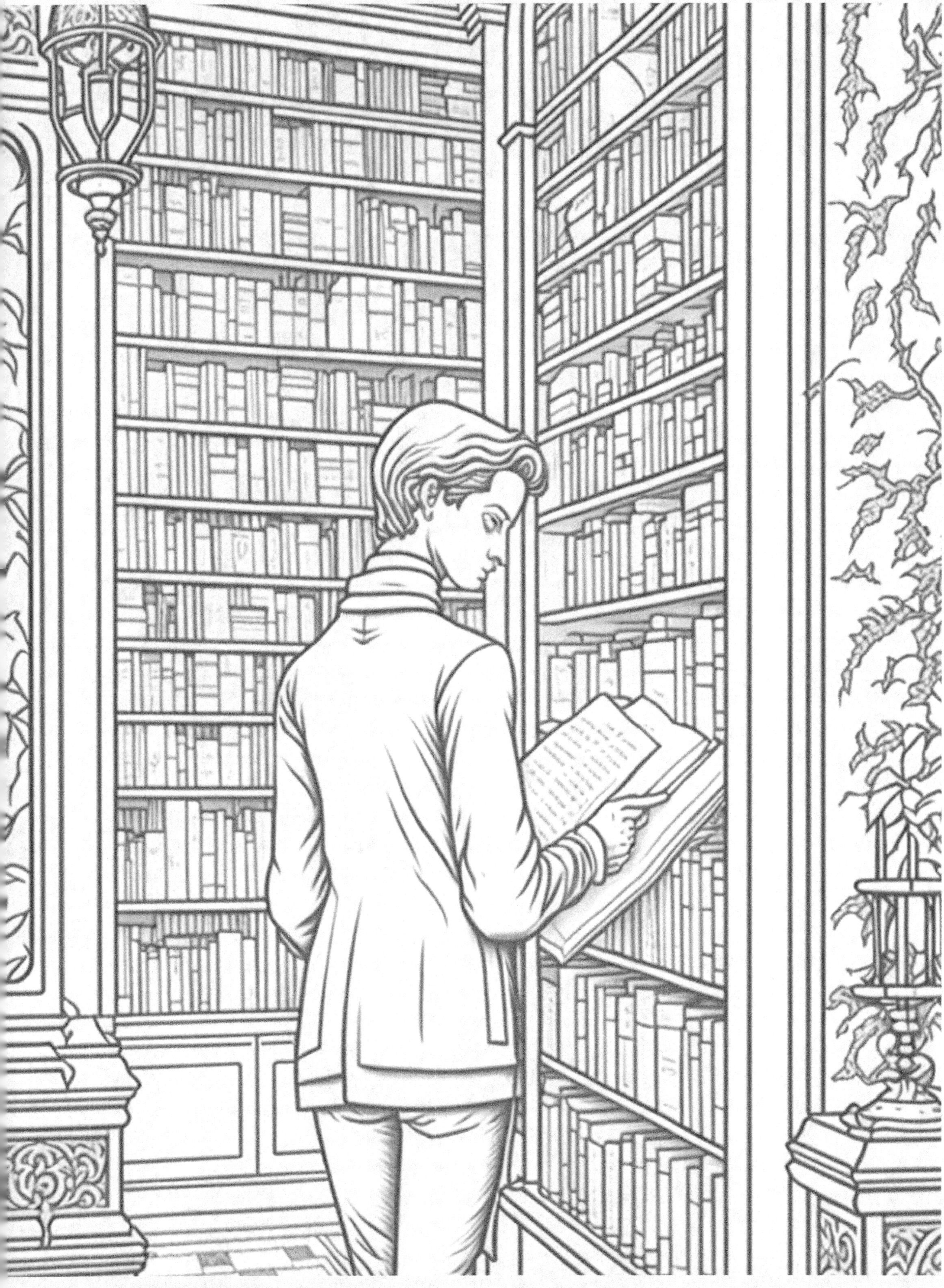

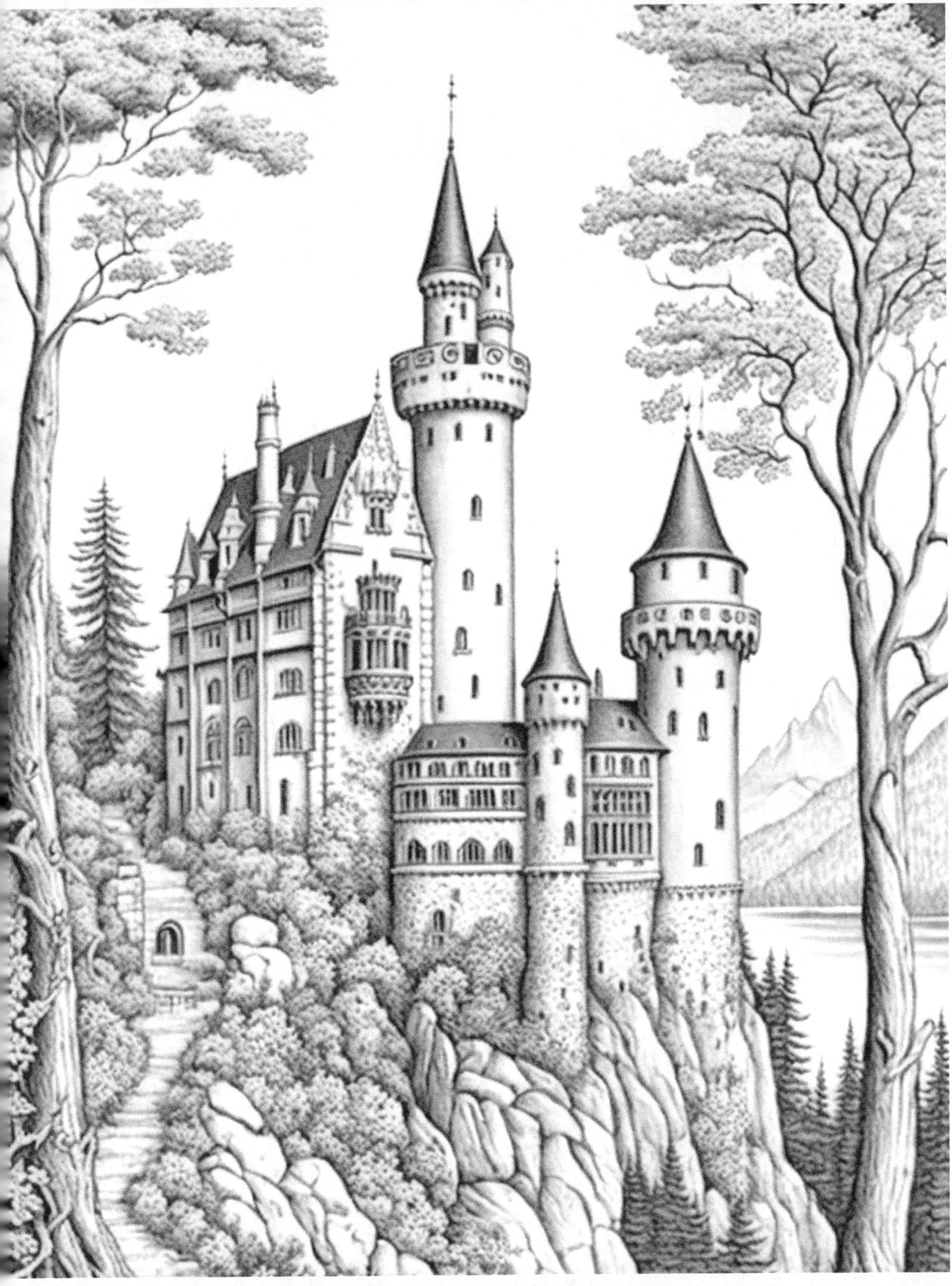

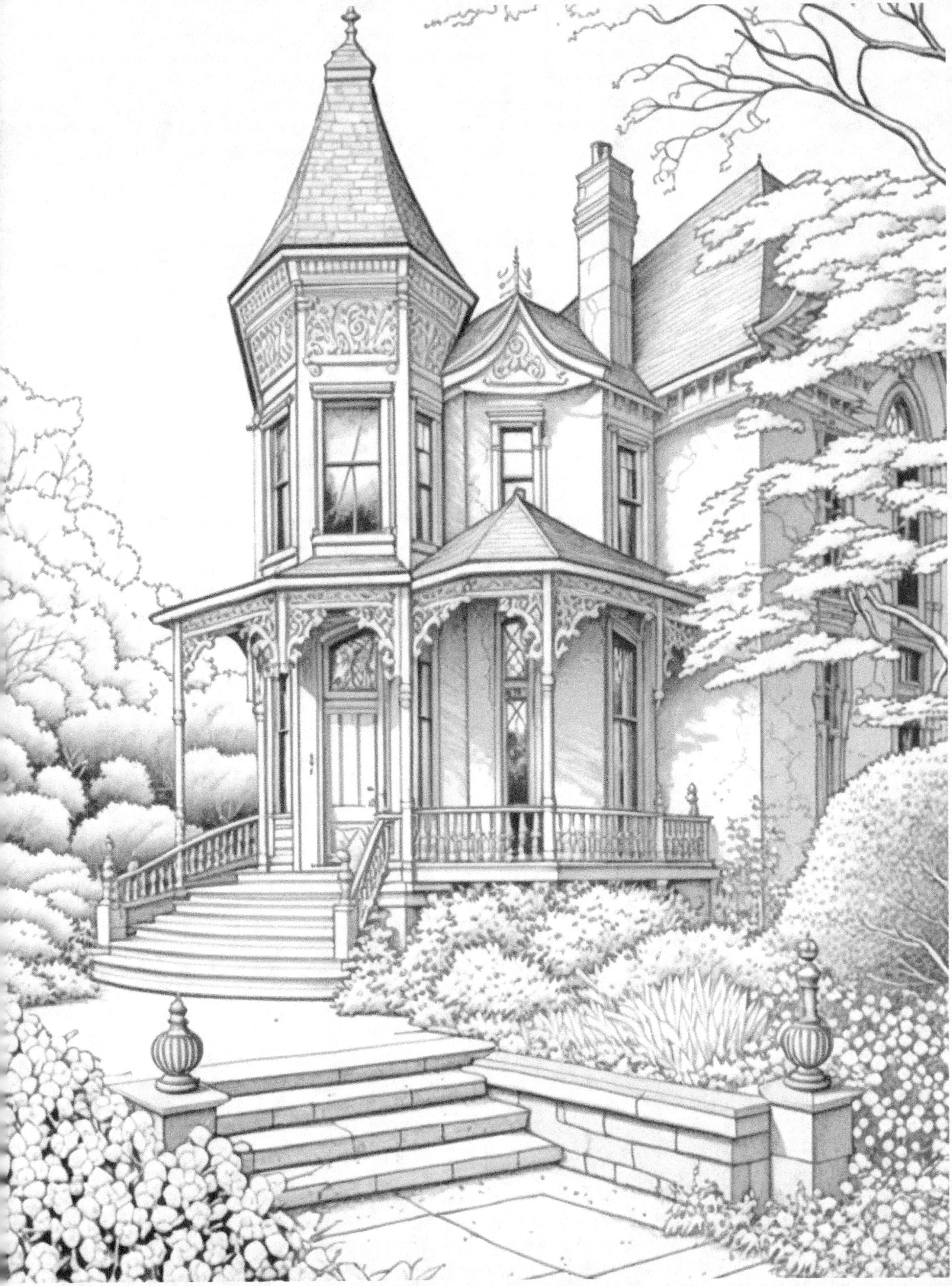

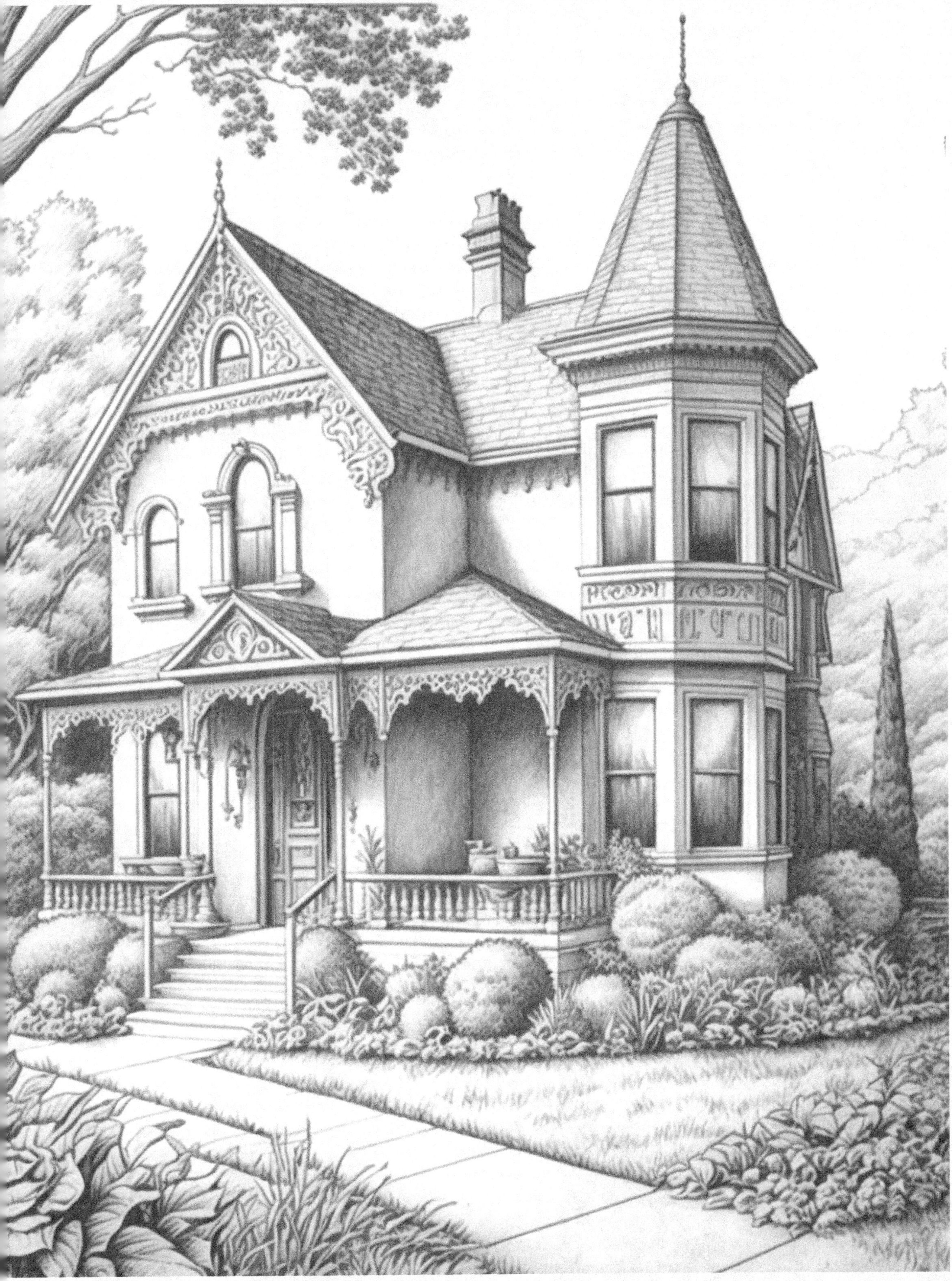

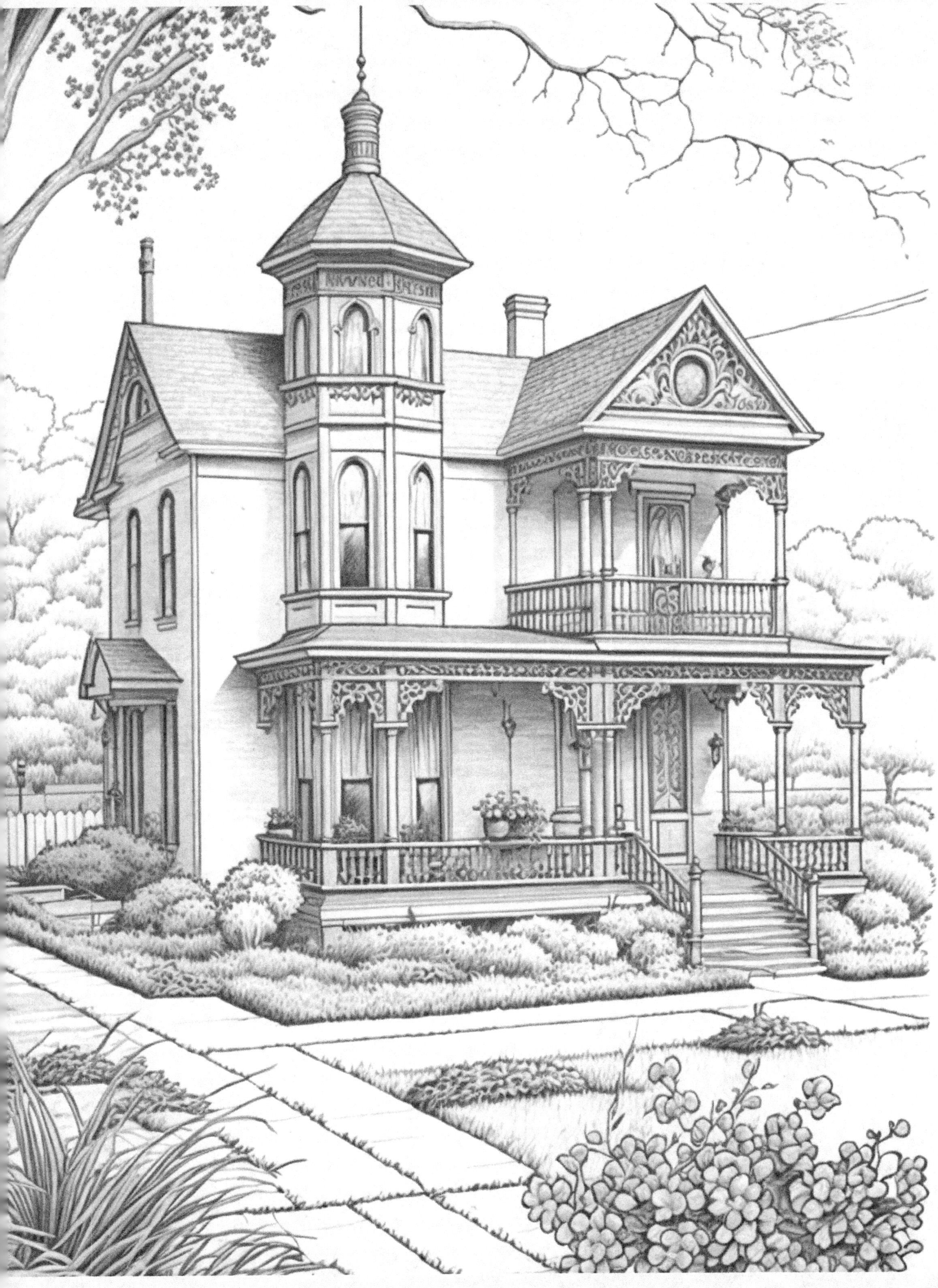

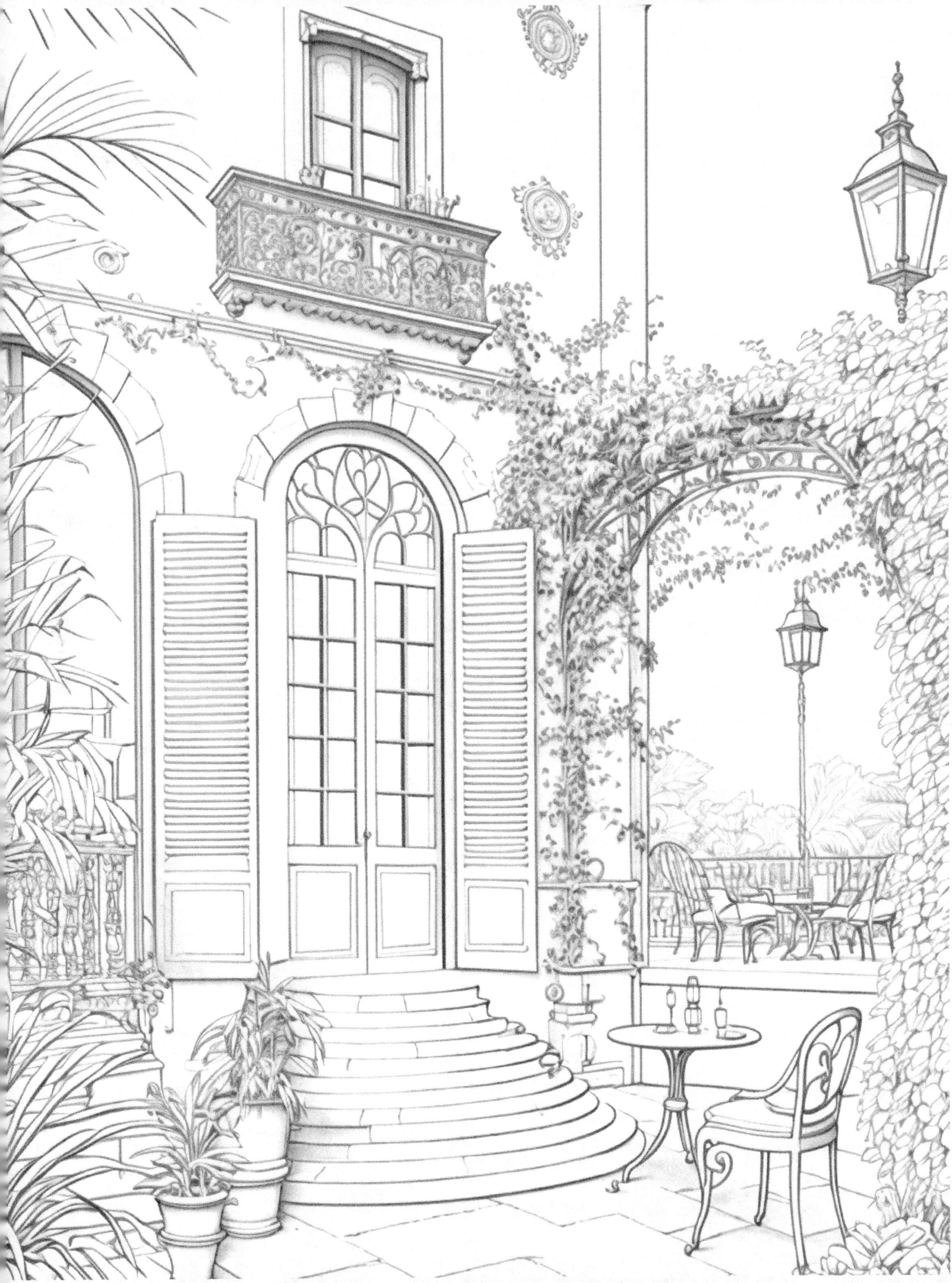

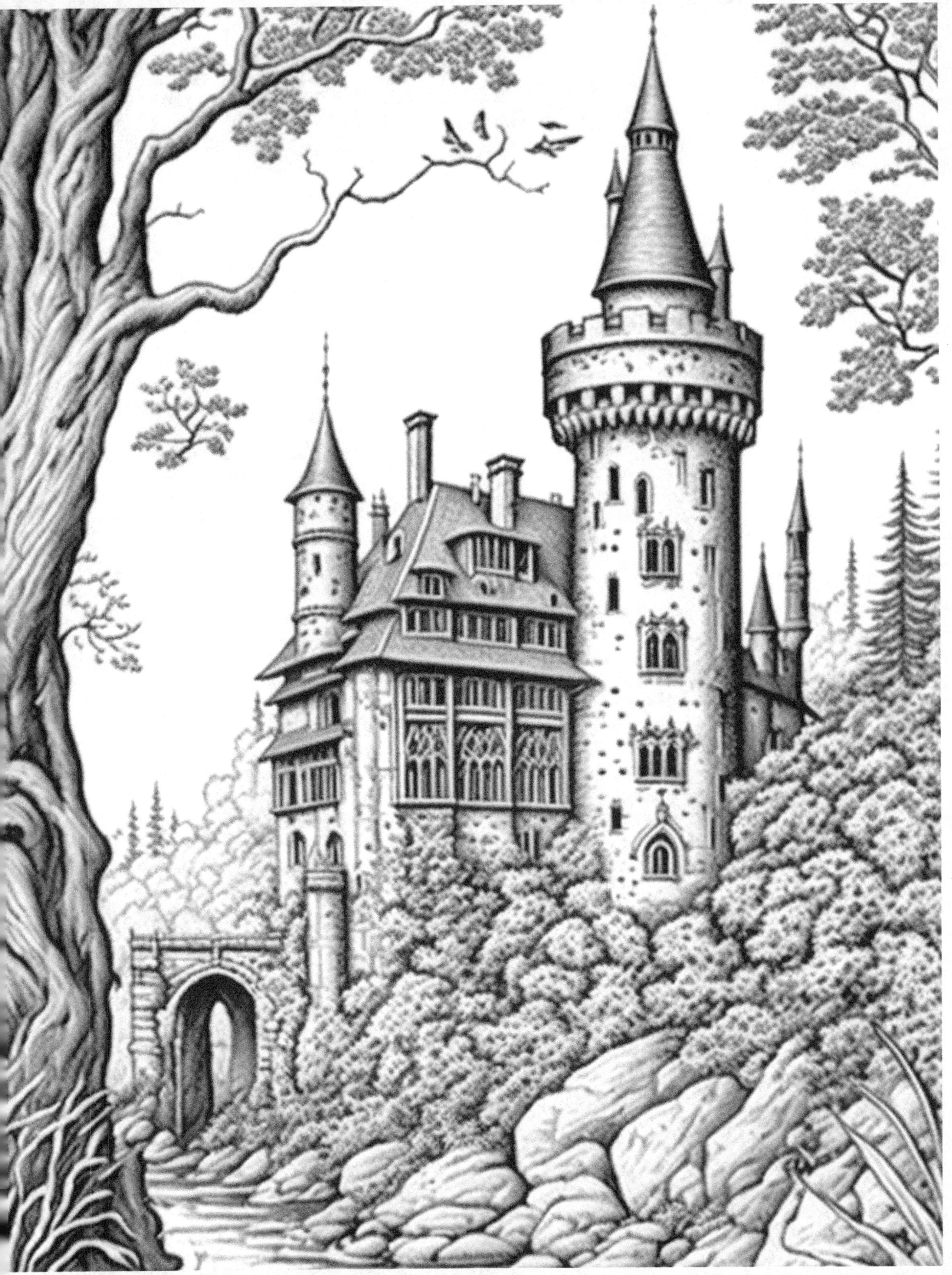

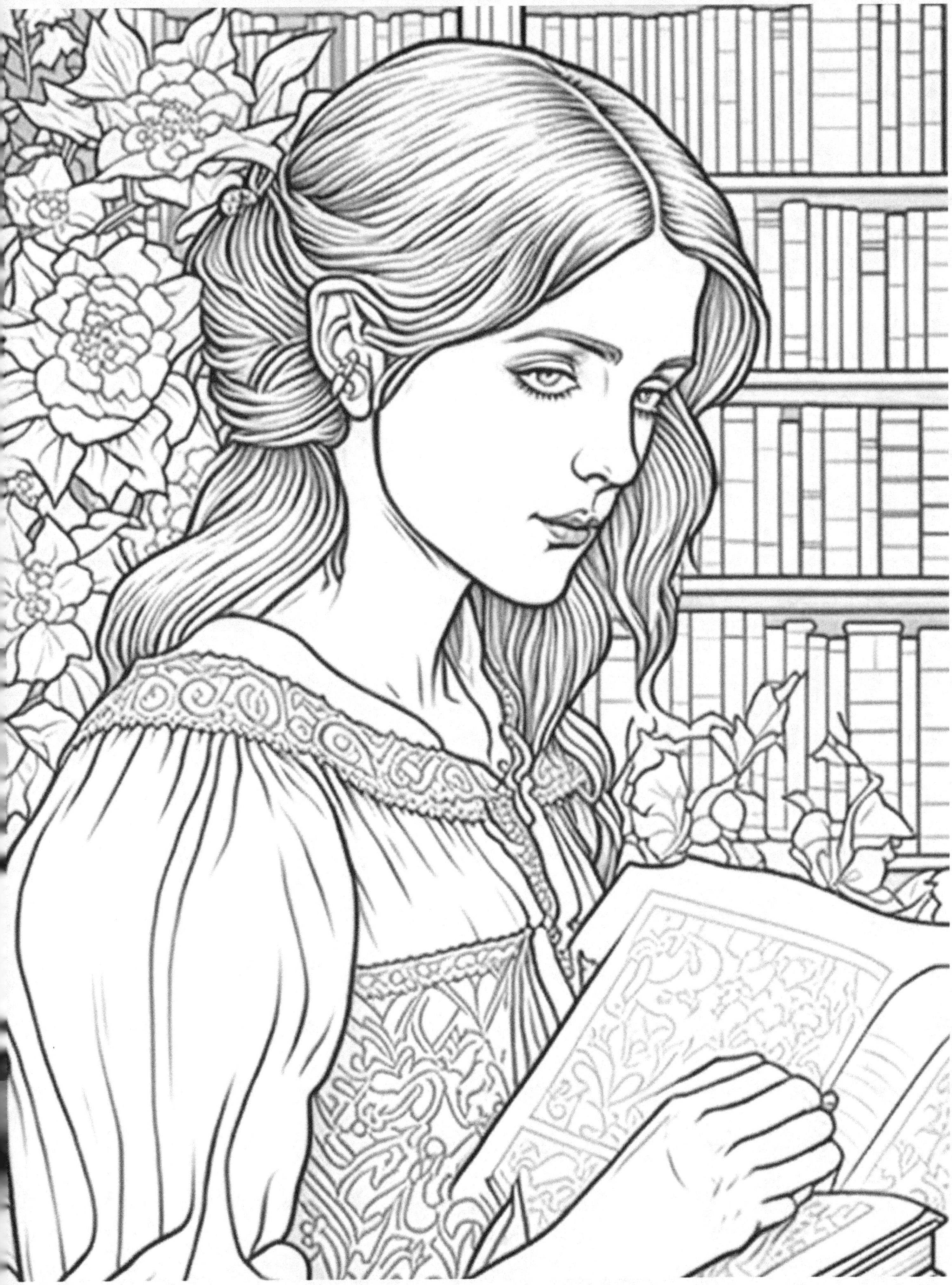

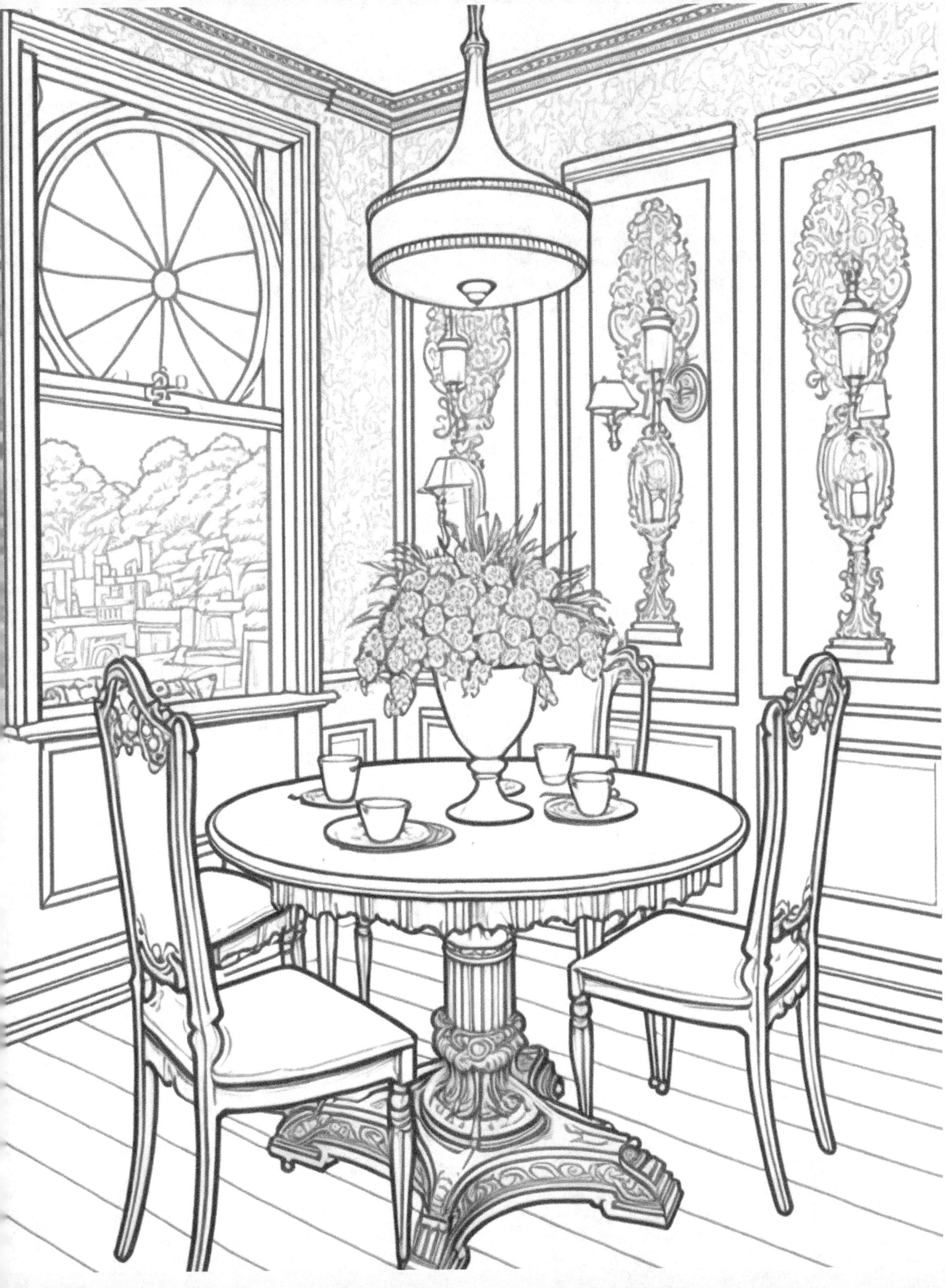

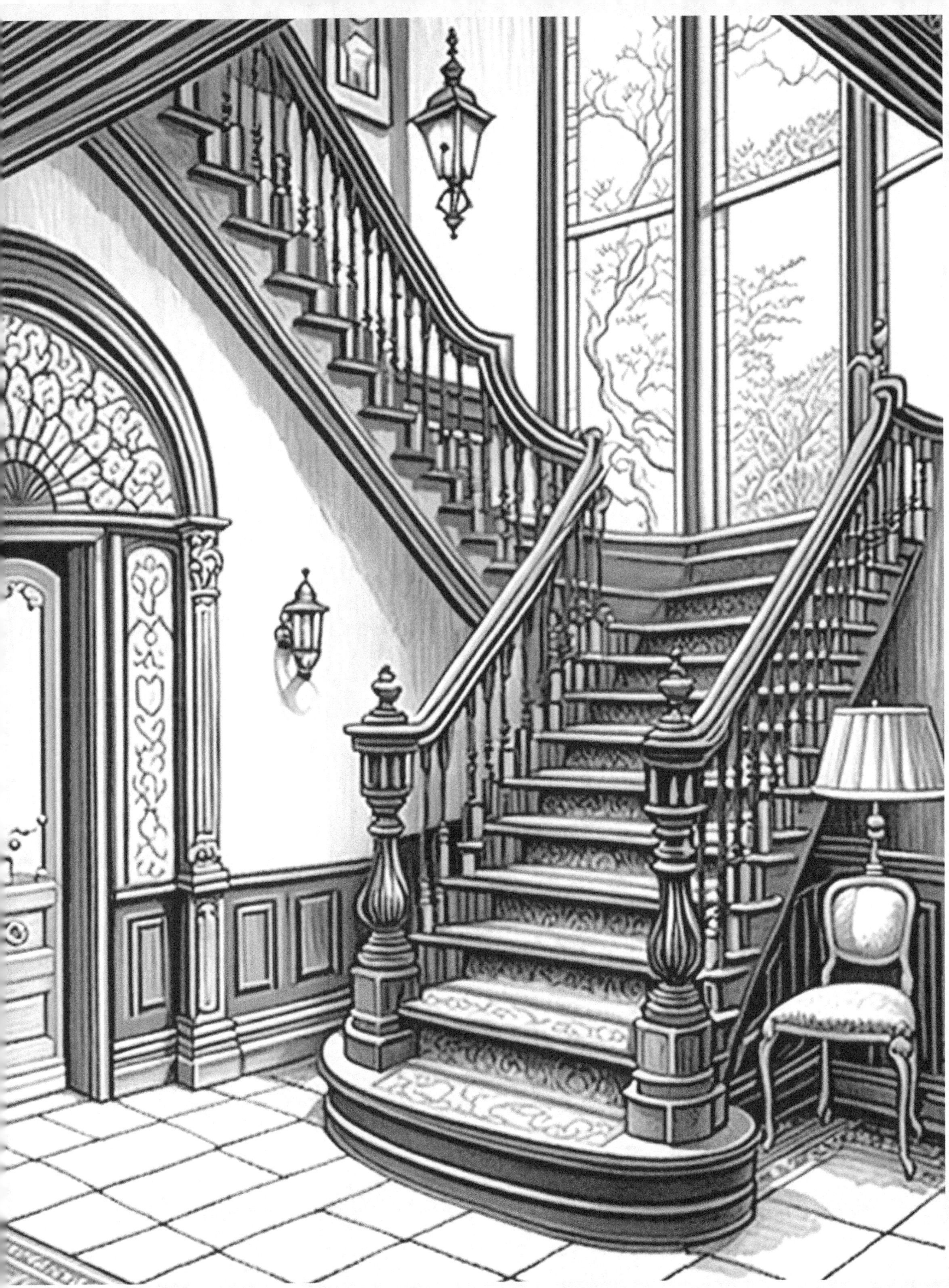

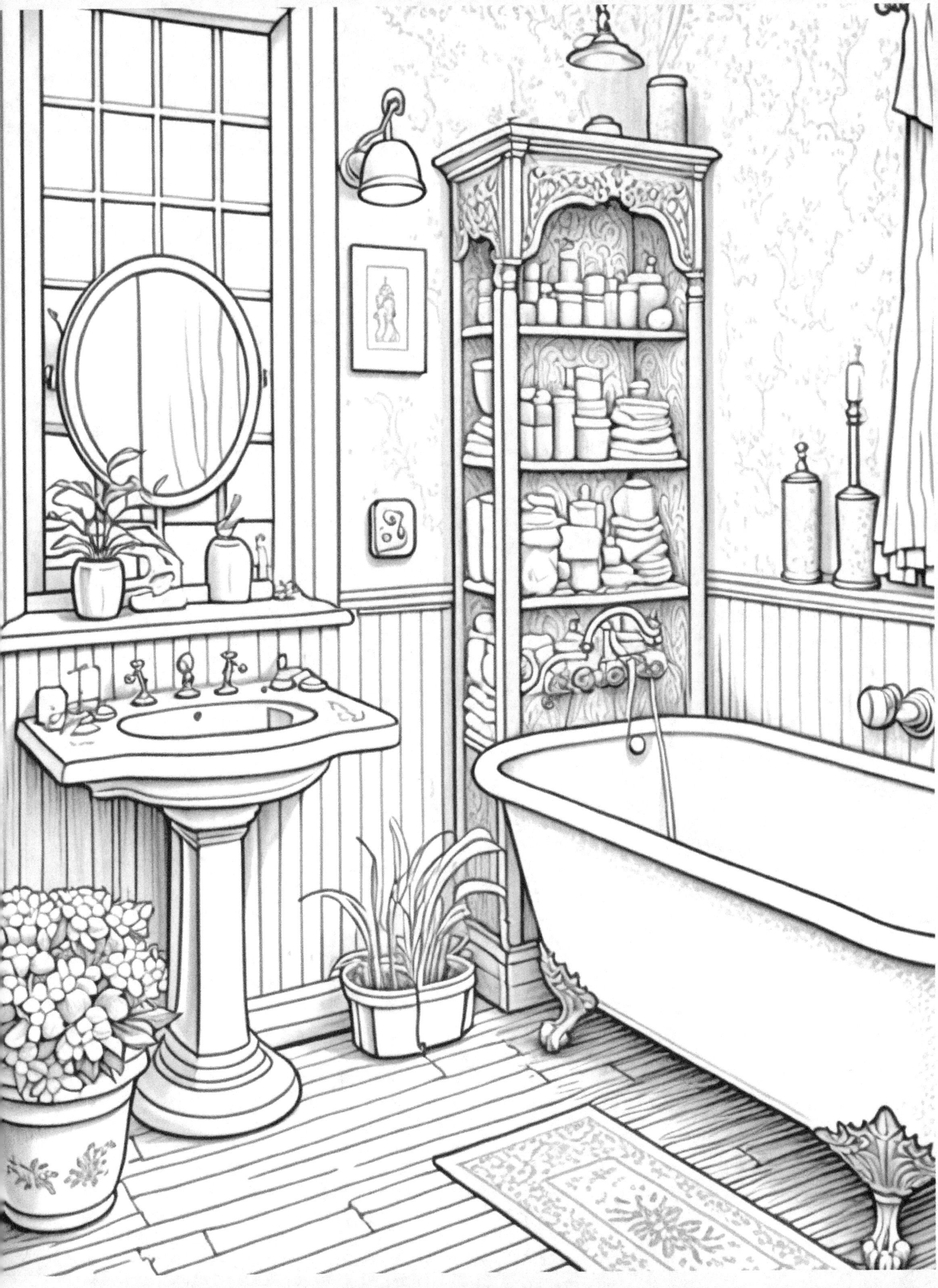

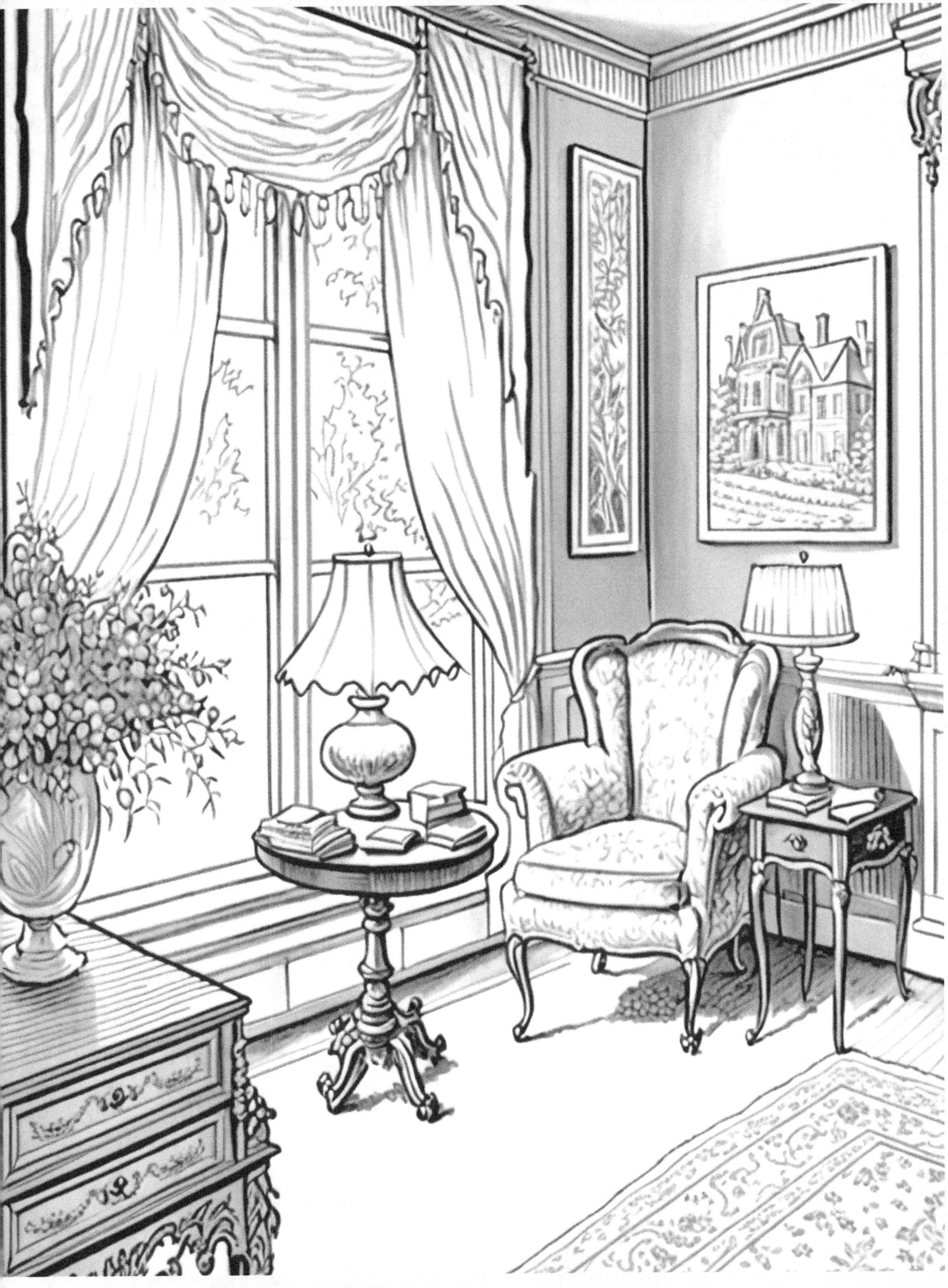

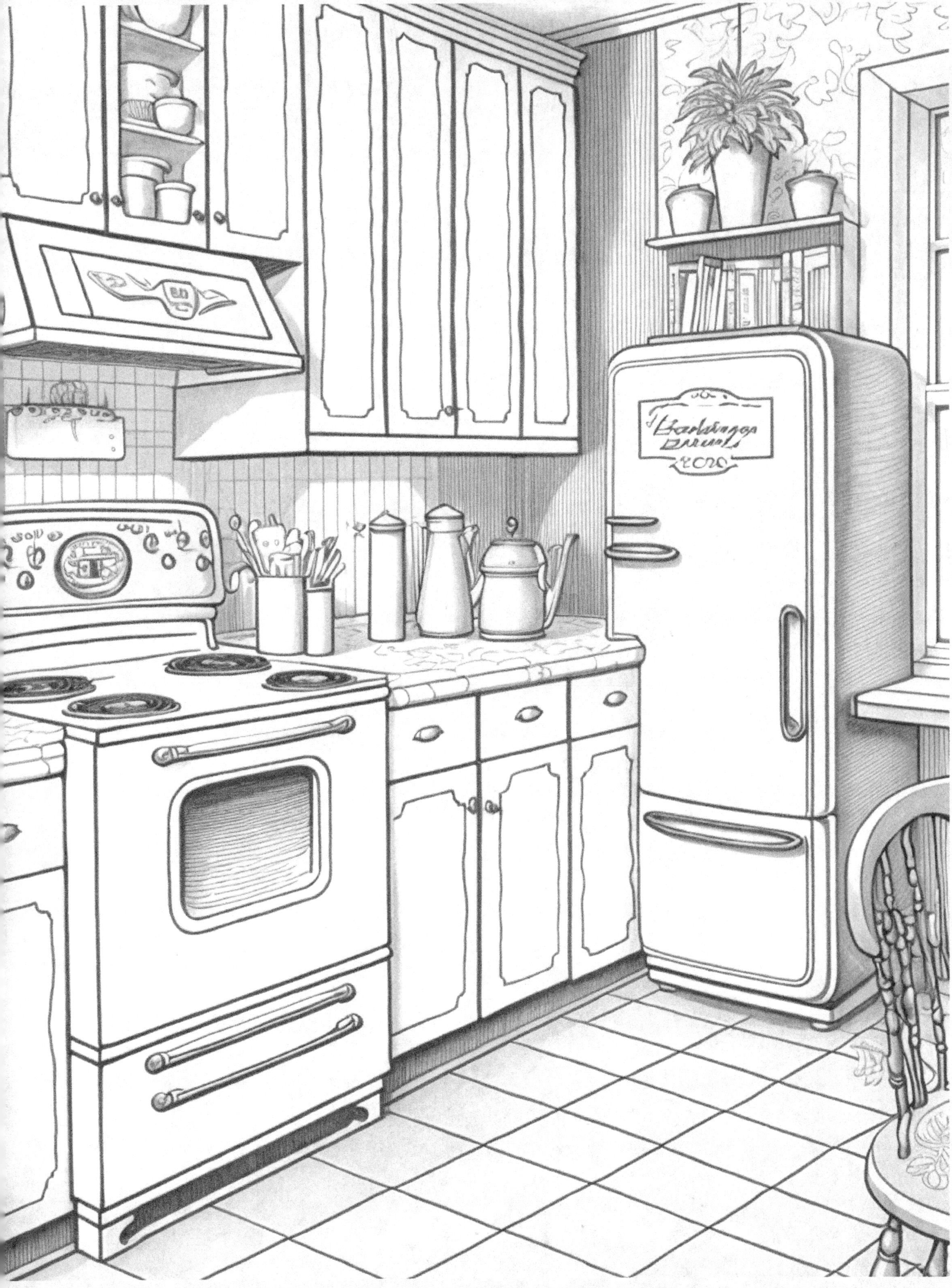

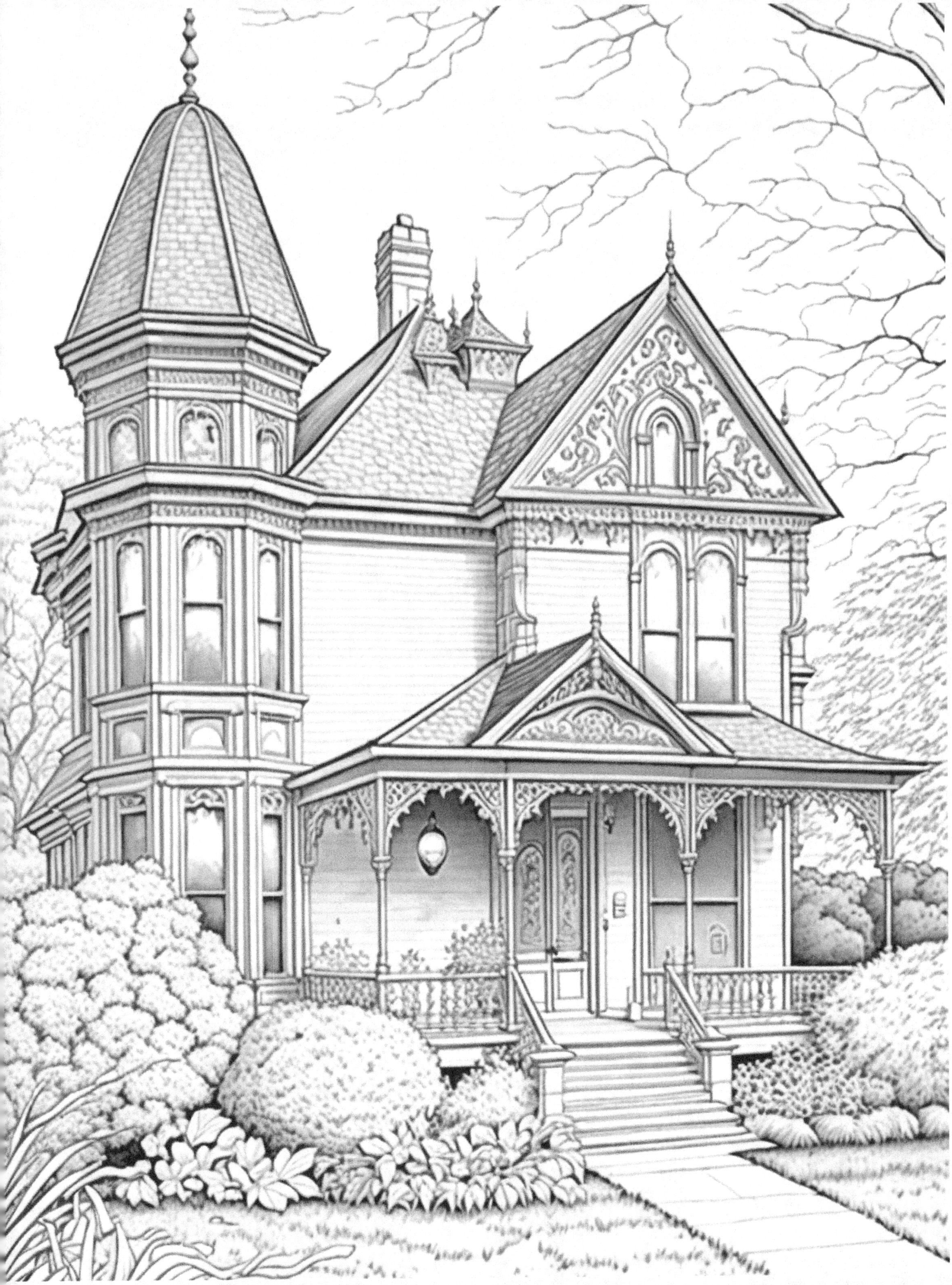

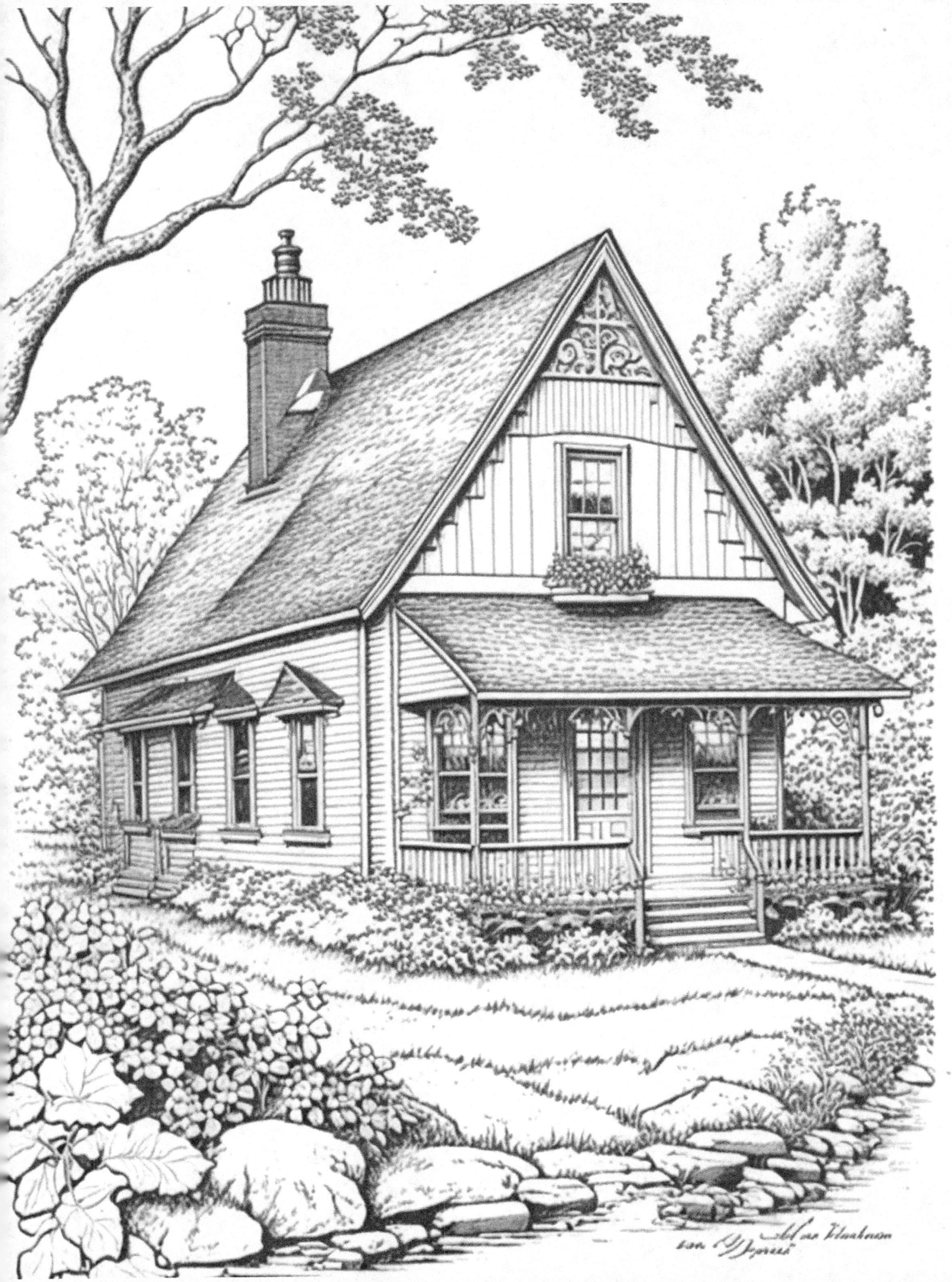

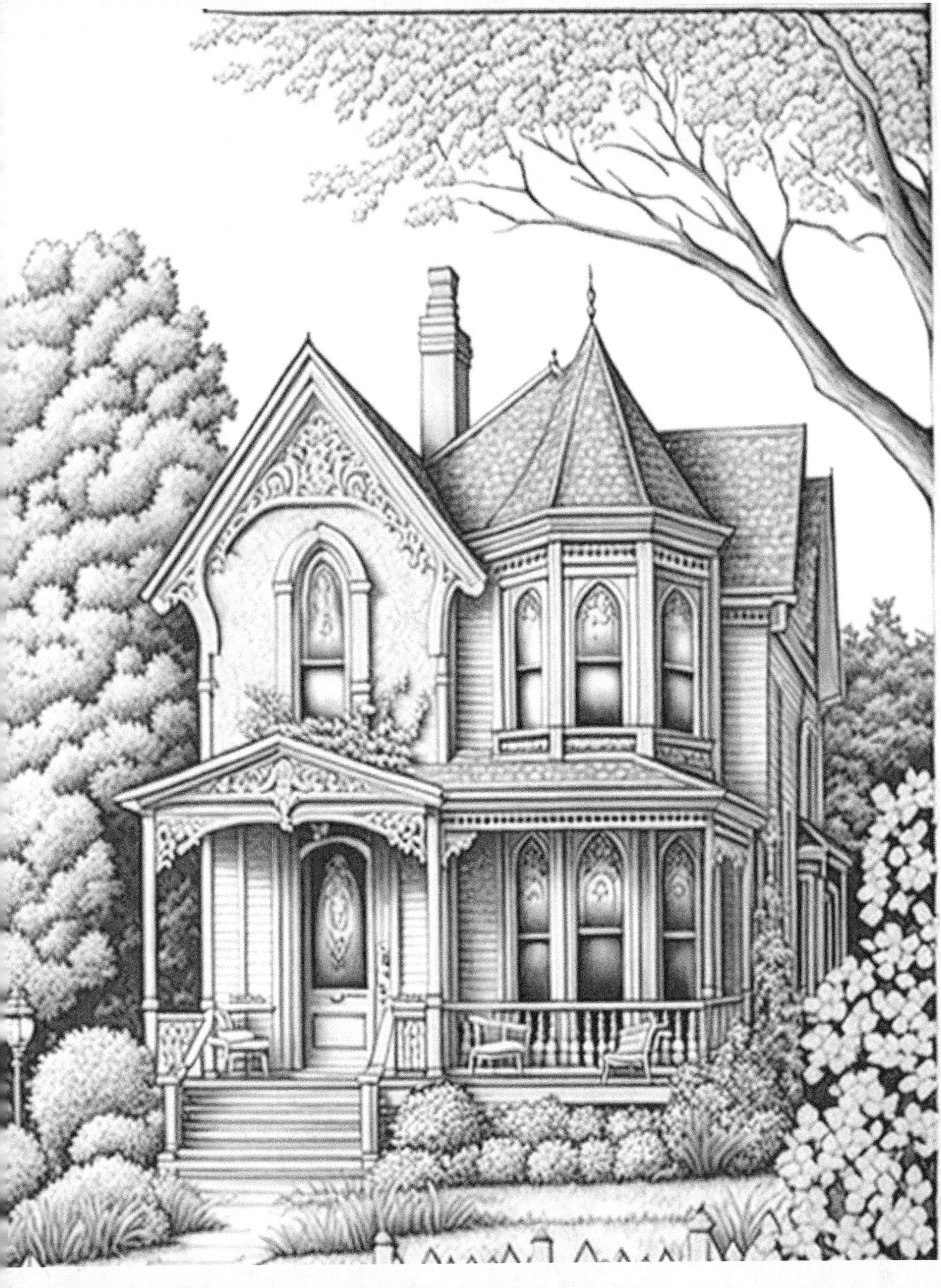

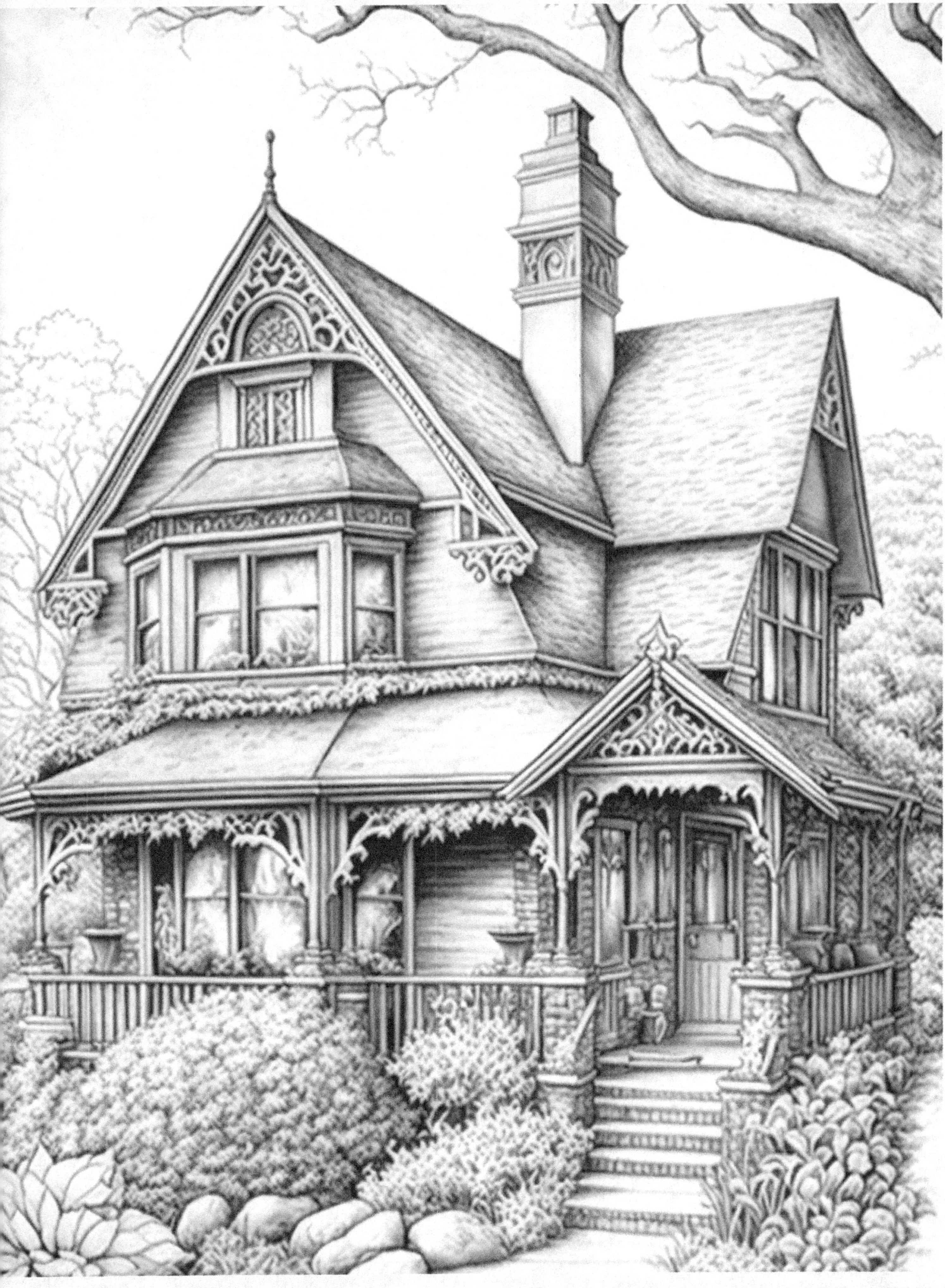

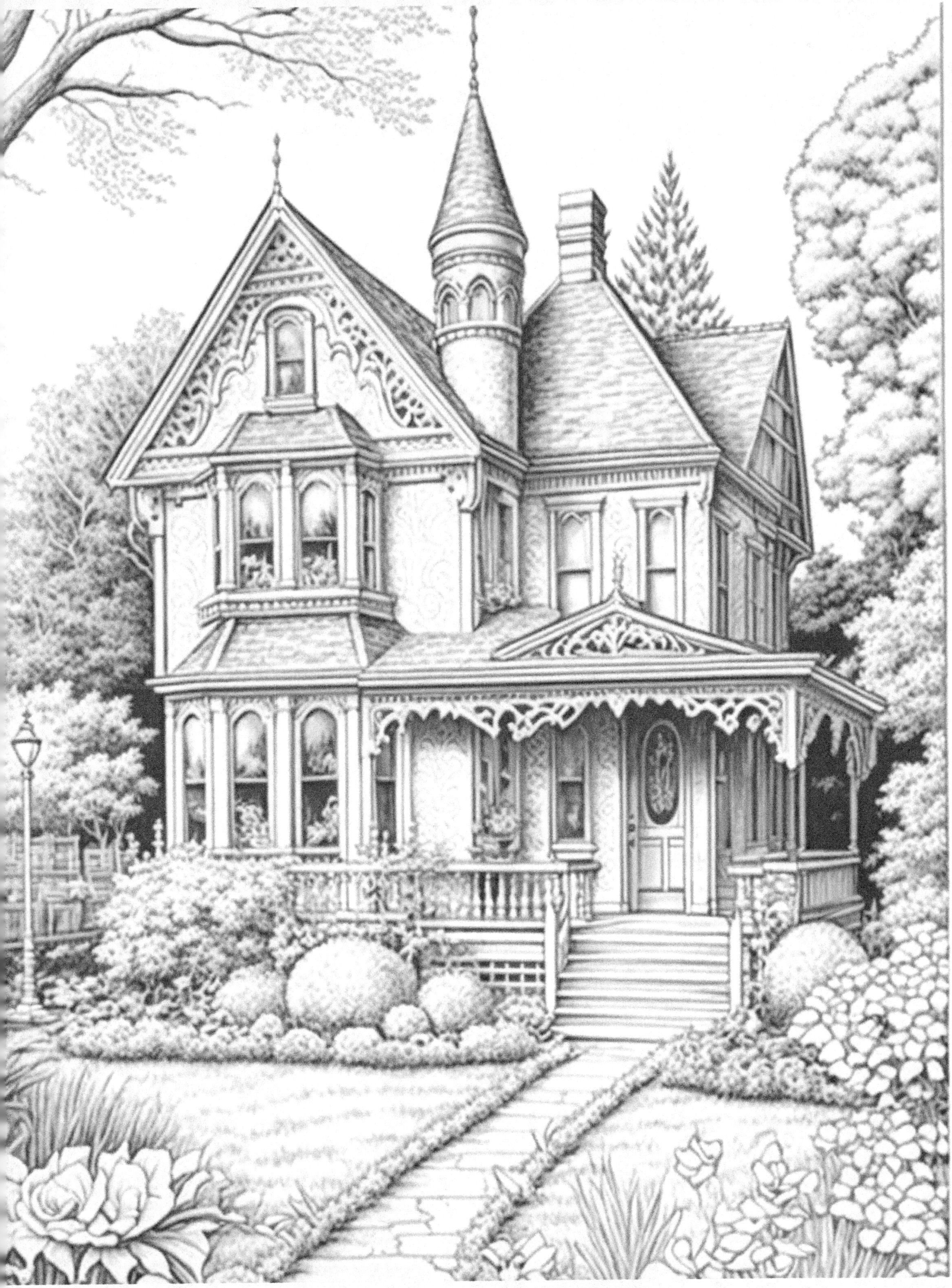

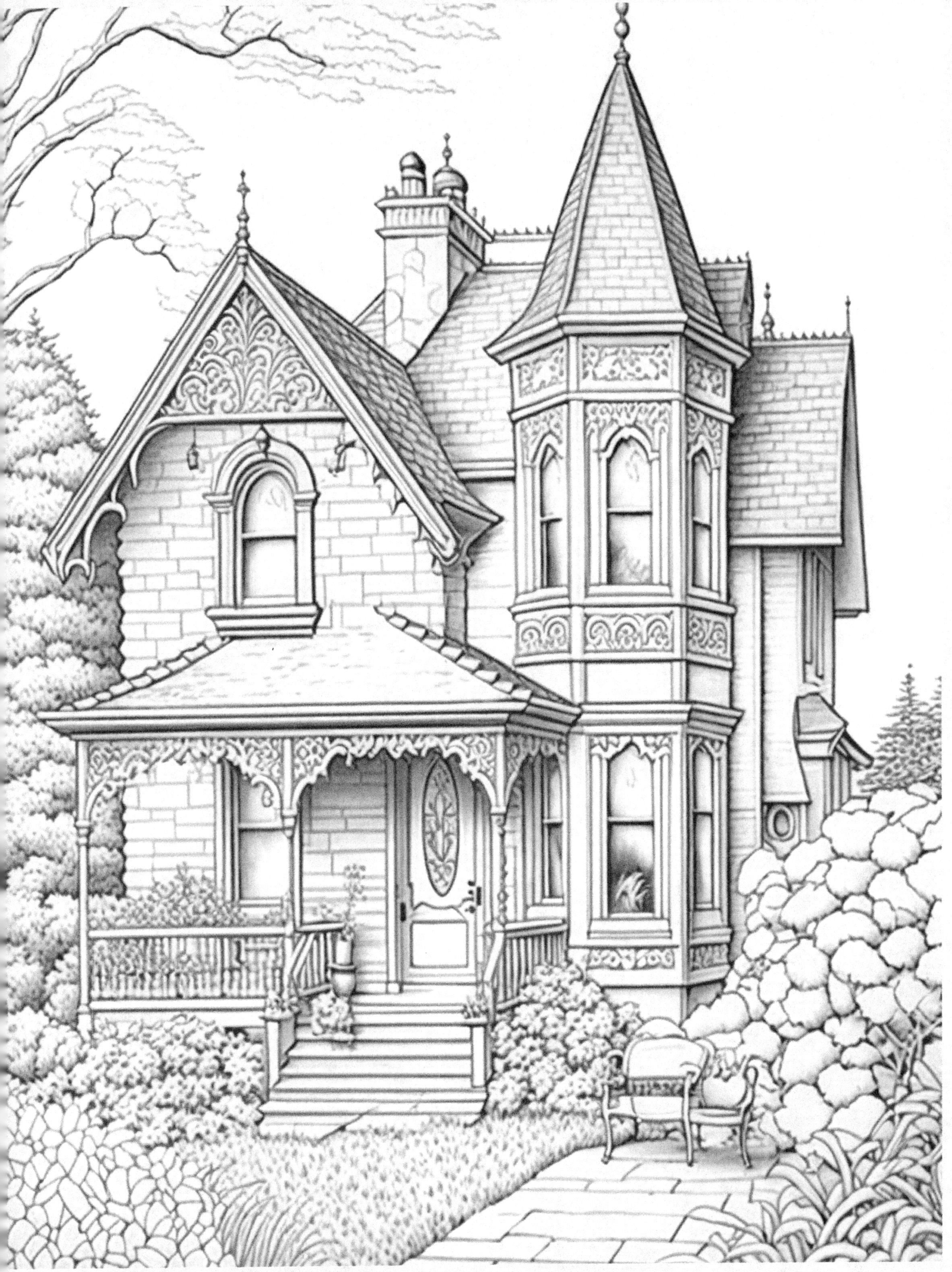

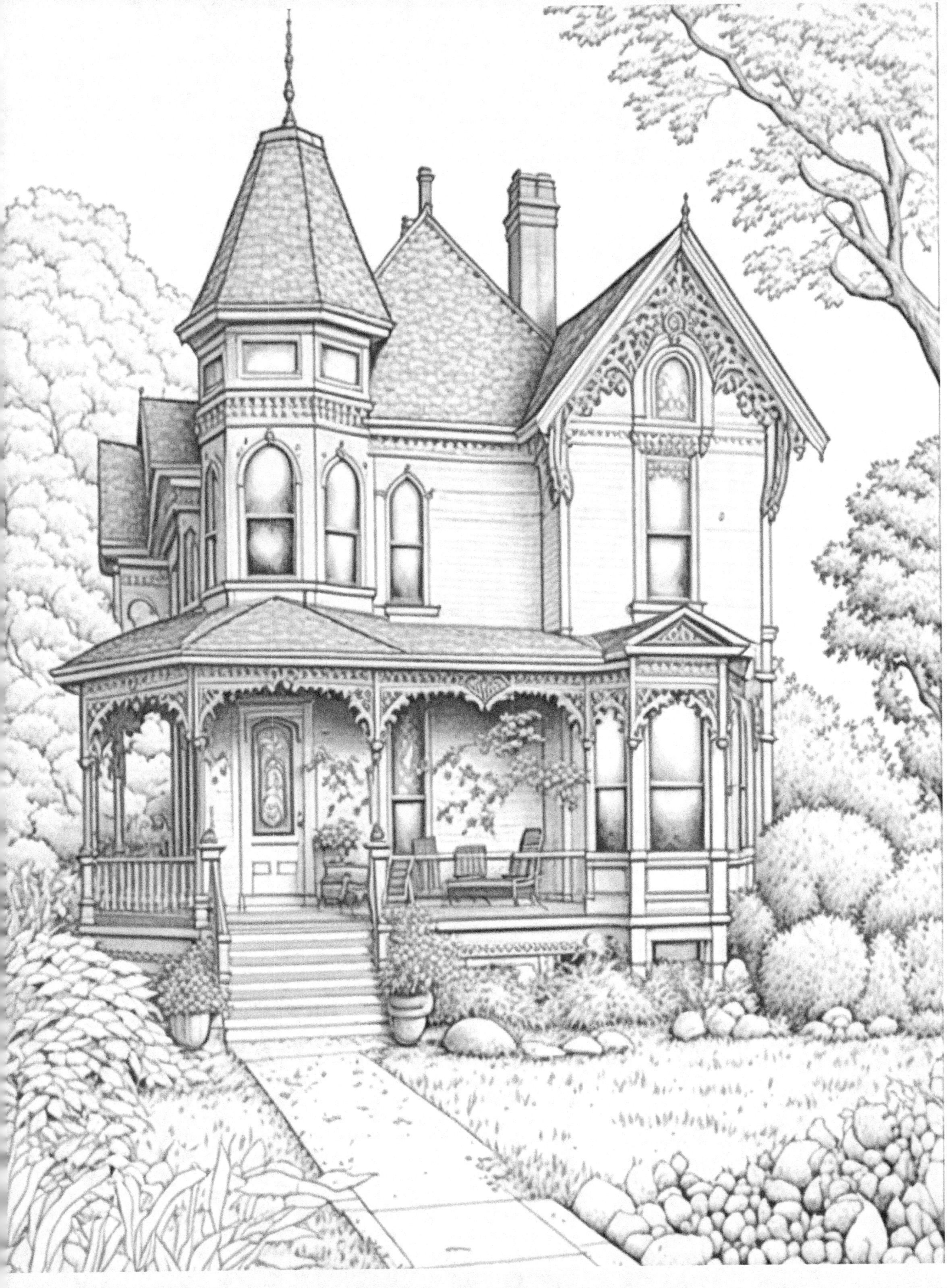

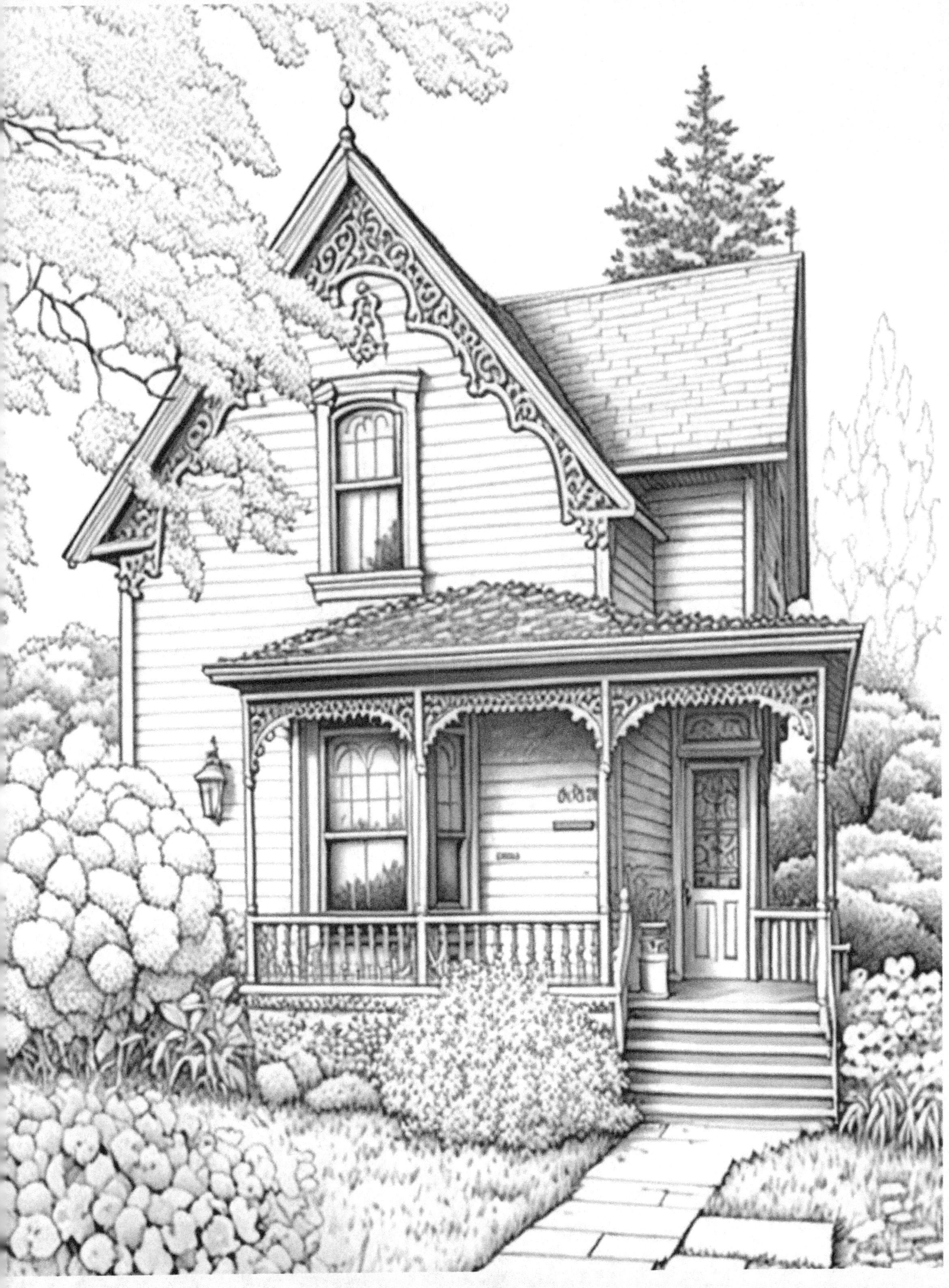

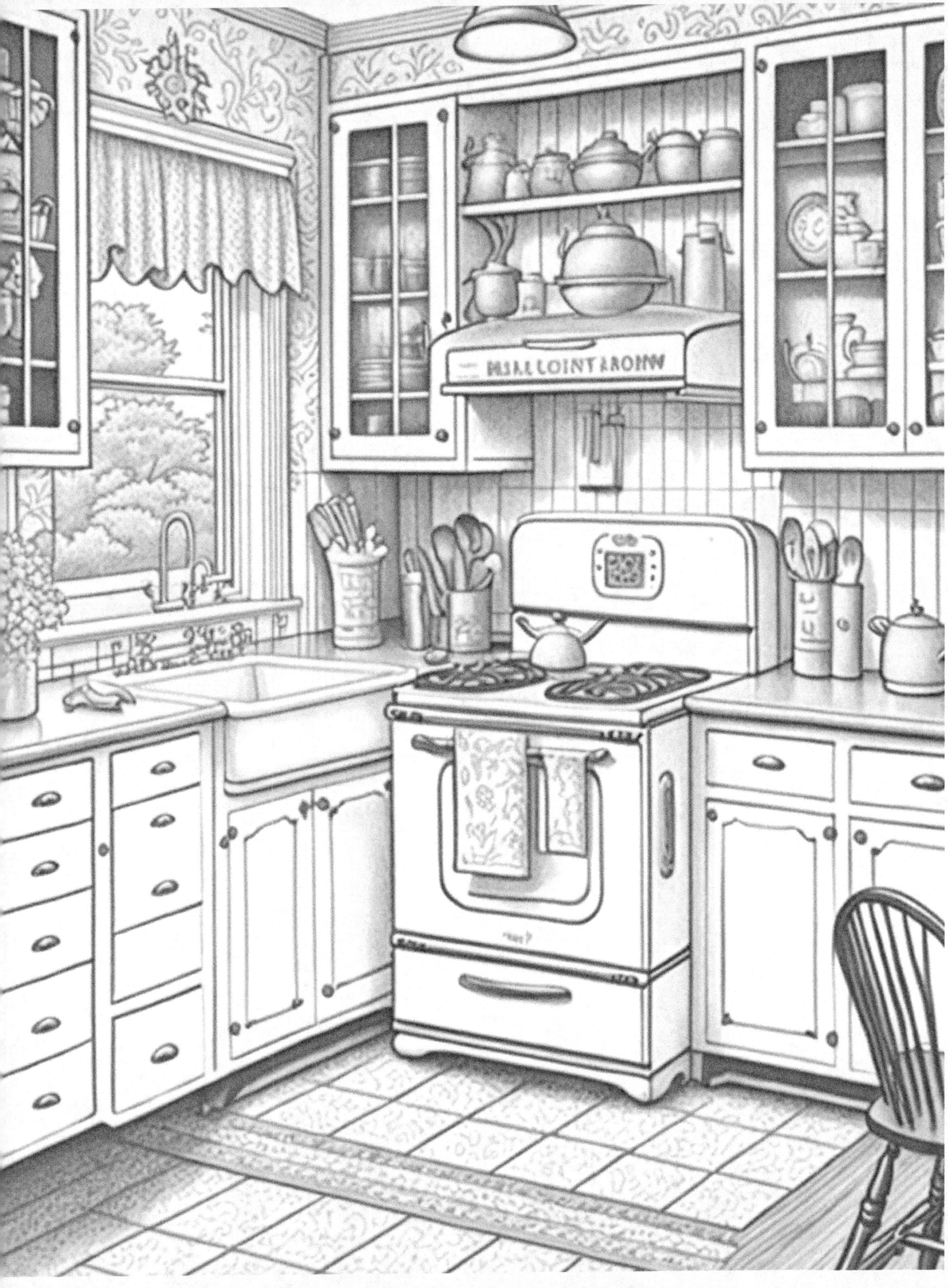

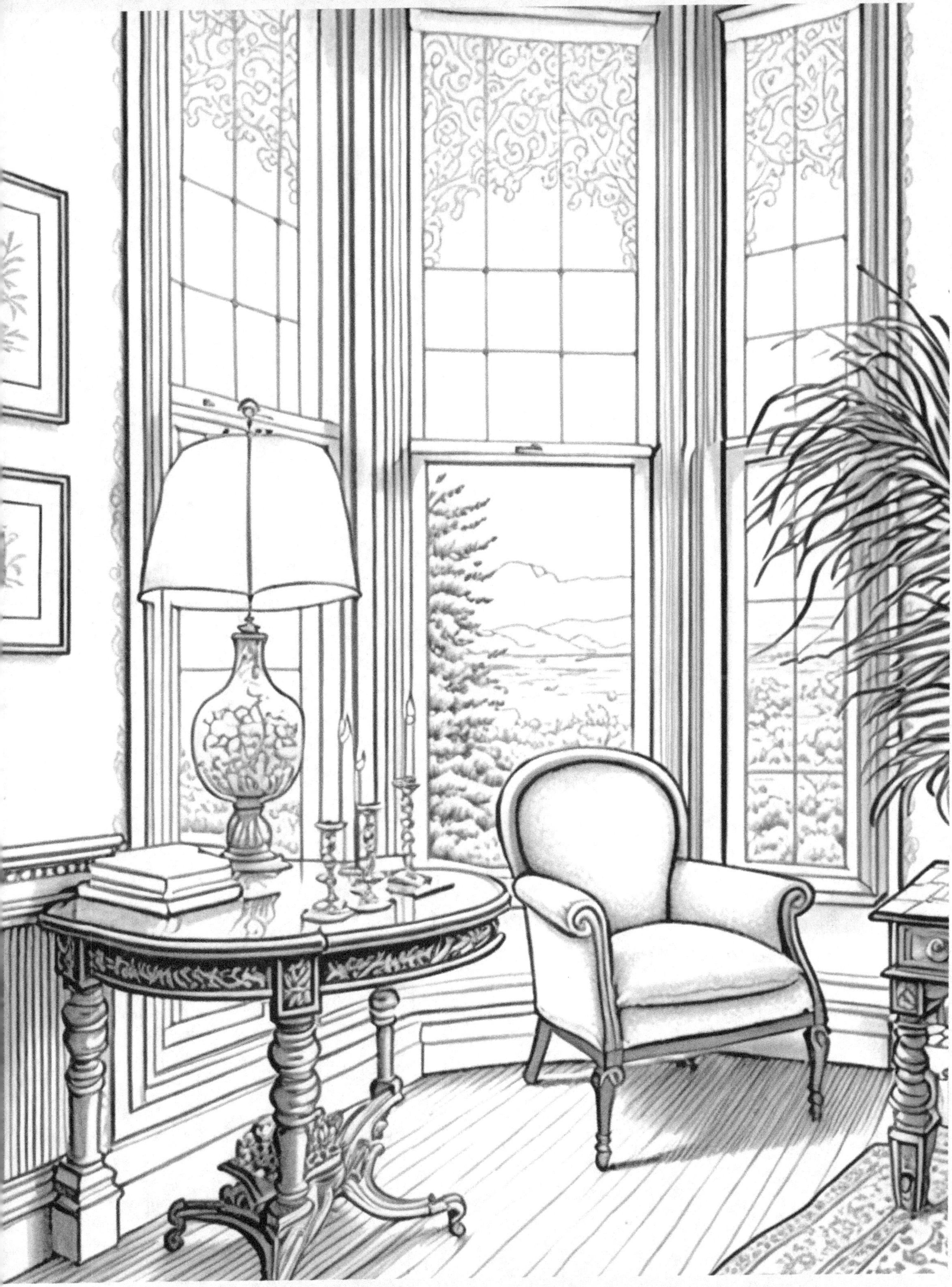

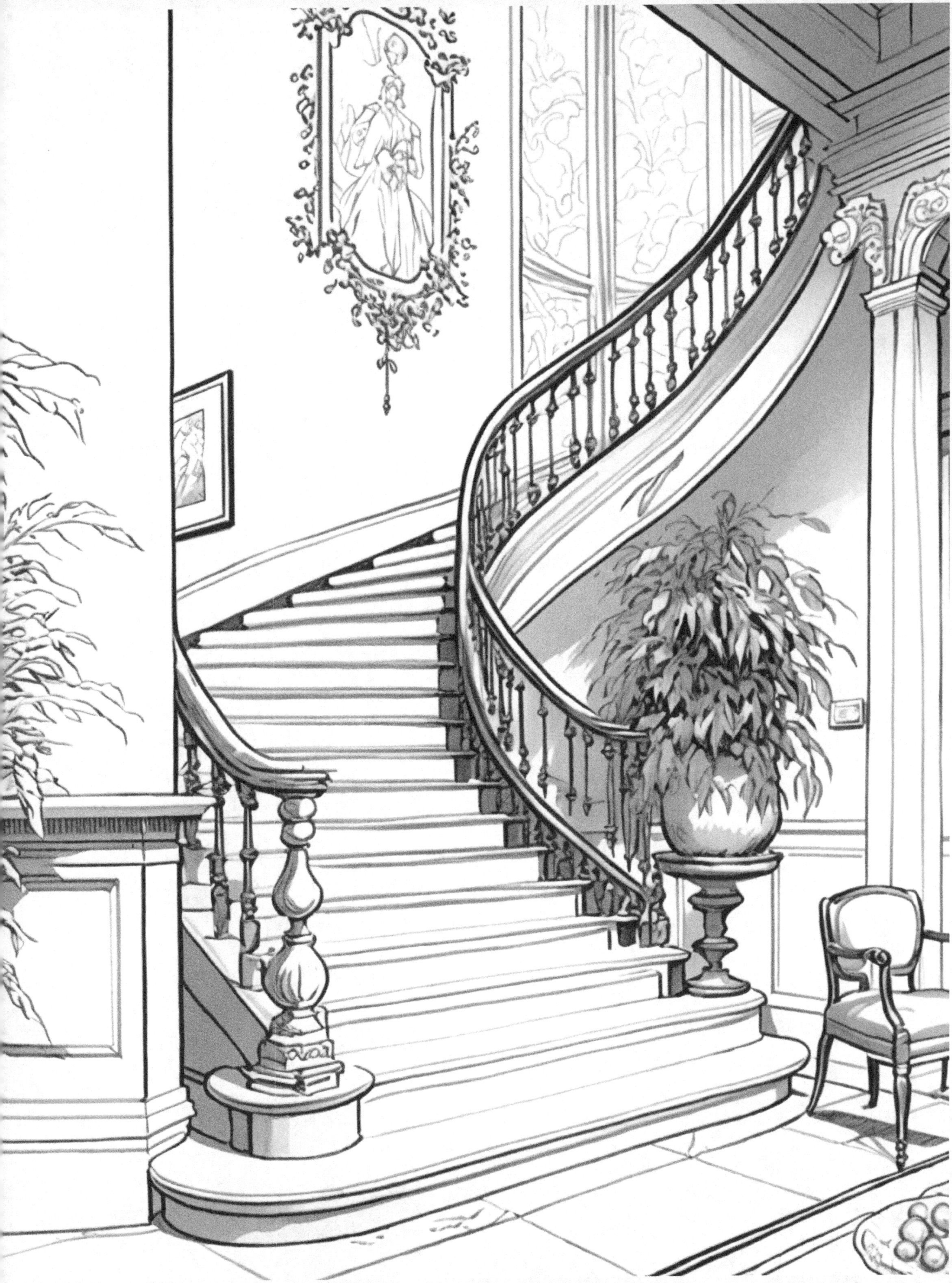

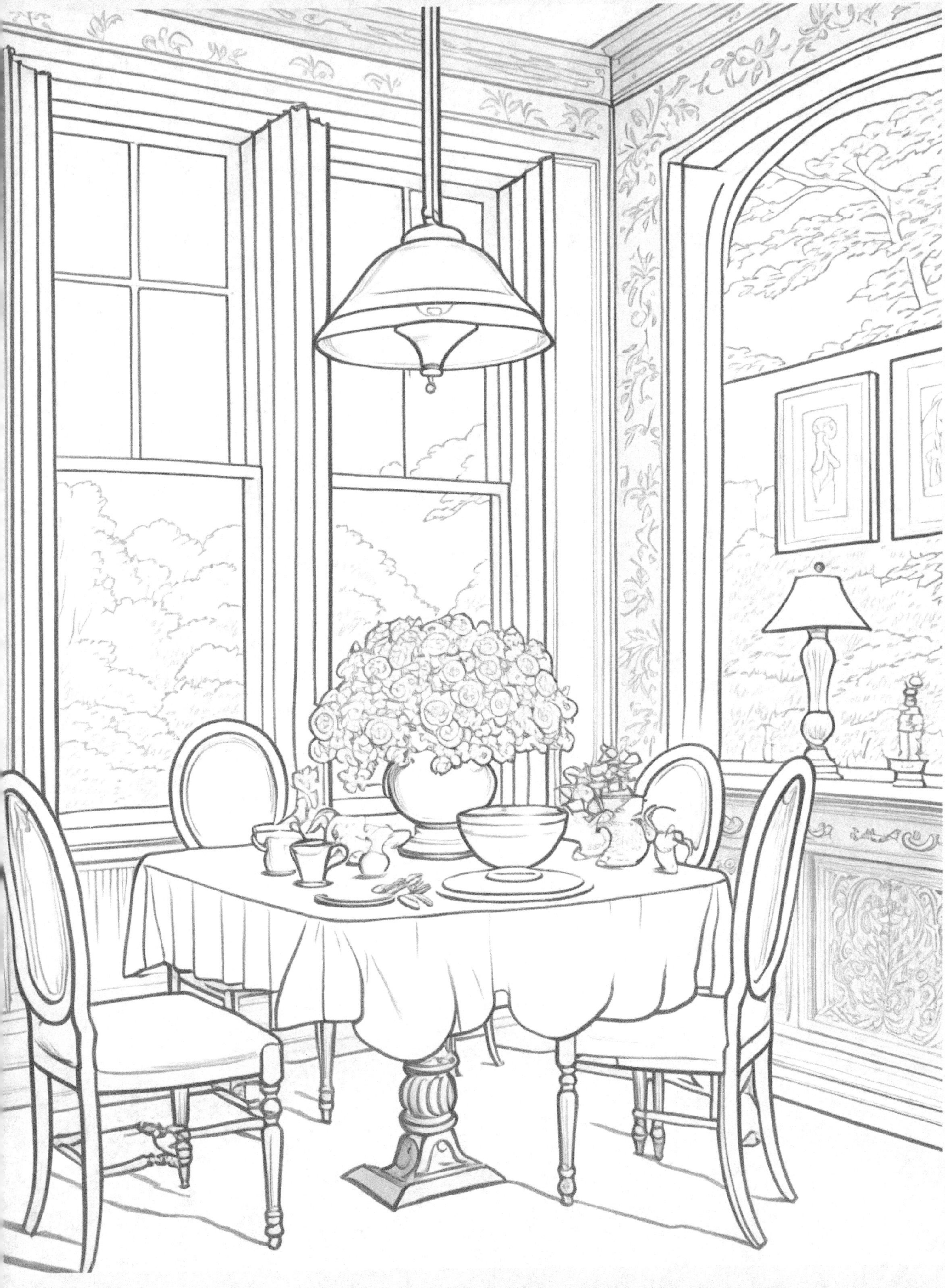

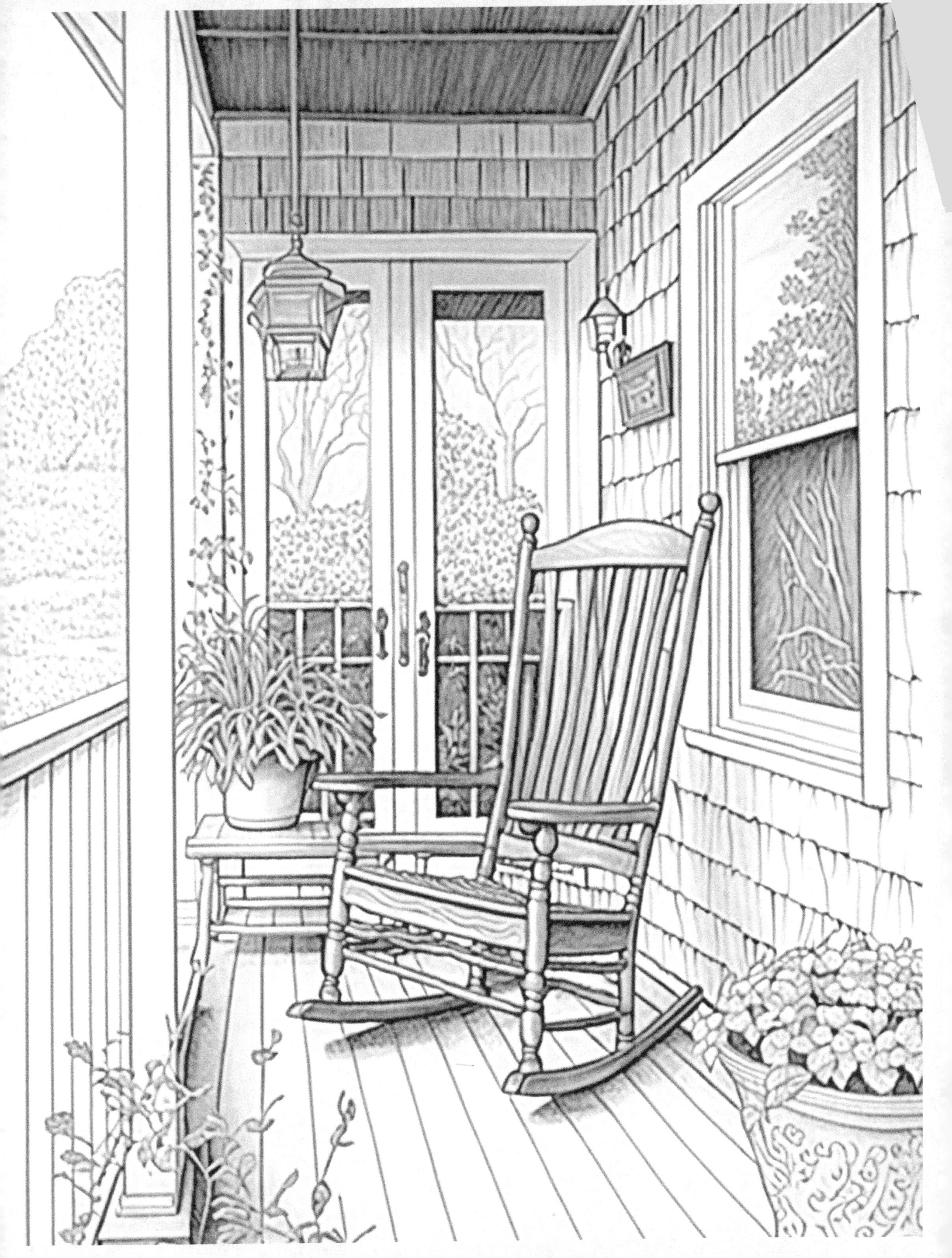